P9-CRZ-066

THE INTERVIEW

Modern Applications of Psychology

under the editorship of

Joseph D. Matarazzo

THE INTERVIEW

Research on Its Anatomy and Structure

Joseph D. Matarazzo

Arthur N. Wiens

UNIVERSITY OF OREGON MEDICAL SCHOOL

ALDINE • ATHERTON
CHICAGO & NEW YORK

ABOUT THE AUTHORS

Joseph D. Matarazzo is Professor and Chairman of the Department of Medical Psychology at the University of Oregon Medical School. He is a Diplomate in Clinical Psychology and has held numerous professional offices at both the local and national levels. Professor Matarazzo has recently completed the revision of the 5th Edition of *Wechsler's Measurement and Appraisal of Adult Intelligence*.

Arthur N. Wiens is Professor of Medical Psychology and Director of Clinical Training at the University of Oregon Medical School. He is a Diplomate in Clinical Psychology, and has held numerous professional offices at both the state and national levels.

First published 1972 by
Aldine • Atherton, Inc.
529 South Wabash Avenue
Chicago, Illinois 60605

ISBN 0-202-26068-2
Library of Congress Catalog Number 72-78225

Printed in the United States of America

Preface

Research on the interview and other two-person communicational interactions has accelerated during the past decade. We and our colleagues have been involved in a program of research in this area, publishing the results of the separate studies in a variety of scientific journals. In view of the burgeoning interest in this field and at the suggestion of colleagues and beginning investigators throughout the country, we decided to attempt to describe this program of research between the covers of one book. This volume is, therefore, a summary of a research program that began in 1954 and is still ongoing. The book reviews the work conducted with a number of colleagues whose names appear in the text and bibliography. Although the interview is the single most frequently utilized technique in all of the communications professions, very little empirical information on this two-person interactional system exists. It is the hope of the authors that the research reviewed here, their own as well as that of other investigators, constitutes another small step toward remedying this deficit.

Writing of the manuscript was completed with the help of a research grant (1297–67) sponsored by the Air Force Office of Scientific Research, Office of Aerospace Research, United States Air Force. All of the content studies reported in Chapter 6 were supported by the same Air Force grant and a grant (GM–1495) from the National Institutes of Health. The earlier studies reviewed in this volume were supported by research grants (M–1107, M–1938, and NU–00133) from the National Institutes of Health, U. S. Public Health Service.

Contents

1

Historical Antecedents of Interview Speech Research

The number of humans now living on earth is estimated at approximately 3.5 *billion*. If one were to add up all the conversations between any two persons in this total, the resulting number of probable two-person conversations occurring in any given hour would be staggering. There probably are thousands of pairs of individuals engaged in conversation within a short radius (miles or possibly even yards) of the reader of this page. In view of the astronomical numbers of daily occurring conversations, it is surprising how little is known about the basic nature of such human conversation, how little it has been exposed to scientific analysis and scrutiny. We propose to introduce the reader to some of the research in this field.

Excellent reviews of selected aspects of this subject have already appeared. Marsden (1965, 1971); Holsti (1968); and Kiesler (in press) have reviewed numerous studies that have investigated the *content* of two-person interviews and conversations: *what* people discuss while conversing. Several excellent articles also have appeared that review related studies in which one conversational partner attempts to control or influence, through a methodology called *verbal conditioning,* the actual *content* of his conversational partner (Krasner, 1958, 1971; Salzinger, 1959; Greenspoon, 1962; Spielberger, 1965; Kanfer, 1968; Heller and Marlatt, 1969). In addition, Flanagan (1965) has reviewed studies on the *physical qualities* of speech—studies involving spectrographic analyses of frequencies (tone), and intensities (volume). Hargreaves and Starkweather (1963) have shown that such spectrographic analysis of speech can be used to establish the identity of individual speakers using these same physical properties of speech alone (that is, yielding "voice prints" akin to fingerprints). Pittenger, Hockett, and Danehy (1960) provide an excellent introduction to still another method of studying speech, namely, through what they term a study of the *paralinguistic* aspects of speech (sighs, slurs, drawls, inhalations, loudness and softness, breathiness, speech coughs, etc.). Finally, Starkweather (1964) has provided an excellent review of additional dimensions of conversational speech such as rate or speed of speaking, reliability of human judgments in studies of speech, judging emotion from a speaker's voice, recognition of speaker identity from voice alone, as well as related variables in human conversation. Since these various reviews already are available in these several references, this discussion will not deal with these topics, but the interested reader is encouraged to consult them for a fuller understanding of these additional dimensions of human speech.

Two Approaches to Studies of Speech

Investigators interested in studying speech, whether occurring in two-person conversations, the focus of our own studies, or occurring in groups of three or more persons, traditionally have focused their investigative interest on either of two facets of such speech: *what* the speaker says or *how* he says it. The first of these two approaches is called *content analysis* and includes study of variables such as frequency of usage of grammatical units (verbs, pronouns, adjectives, and other grammatical units) and themes (references to parents or other significant humans, distress–relief words, past or future tense usage, affectionate or hostile words, so-called manifest or latent meanings, degree of inferred empathy or lack of empathy toward the conversational partner inherent in the statement, anxiety-laden versus neutral themes and topic areas). (See above references to excellent reviews of such content-oriented studies.) The second approach to the study of human speech deals not with *what* is said (content) but, rather, with *how* it is said. Physicists, electronic engineers, experts in acoustics, students of high fidelity sound recording, and others have taken speech (spoken or sung) and have played it into oscilloscopes and other electronic equipment in order to analyze formal components of this kind of speech such as its frequencies, intensities, timbre, and related acoustical qualities. Flanagan (1965) provides an excellent review of this segment (acoustical) of the approach to study of *how* human speech is delivered.

Investigations in a subarea of *how* people speak are often referred to as *content-free* studies, or studies of the *noncontent* dimensions of speech. They also sometimes are referred to as studies of the *formal properties* of speech (for example, studies of frequencies and durations of individual utterance units, interruptions of one's conversational partner, latency before answering him). However, as indicated above, the acoustical variables reviewed by Flanagan also represent formal, noncontent, or content-free properties of speech. We and our colleagues have not conducted any studies in the Flanagan-type analysis of the physical properties of speech. We have limited ourselves to study of frequencies and durations of single units of utterance, latency, and interruption in two-person and multi-person conversational groups.

From the beginning we have been interested in studying the current emotional, attitudinal, or motivational state of our interviewees—in psychotherapy or in other real-life interview encounters. The interested reader will find the miniature theoretical framework, emanating from the work of Chapple (1942), which guided our initial choice of interaction variables described at length in Matarazzo, Saslow, and Matarazzo (1956) and Saslow and Matarazzo (1959).

Defining Basic Units

Difficult as it might be to realize, a major hurdle to research on human speech (whether involving content or noncontent approaches) has been a lack of agreement among investigators on how to define the basic unit or units to be studied. The reader interested in this problem should ask himself how he would go about analyzing in a systematic manner the words written on the page he is currently reading; or, better still, the transcribed employment interview given in the appendix to this volume. After having decided on a category system the reader would next have to ask how he would divide the page of words (or interview) into *units* to apply his (probably content-oriented) category system. Would he simply use single sentences as his unit for analysis? Or shorter phrases? If the latter, how would he decide where one phrase begins and ends? After the reader arrives at an approach that satisfies him, he should ask a friend to carry out the same steps independently. The predictable resulting lack of agreement and confusion, if not downright hostility, between the reader and his friend provides a brief glimpse at what has transpired between serious investigators during the past two decades. Marsden (1965, 1971); Holsti (1968); and Kiesler (in press) have summarized and critically reviewed the major problems in this subarea.

One would expect that reaching agreement on standardized definitions of noncontent properties such as durations of single utterances in spoken conversation would present fewer problems for investigators working in different settings. Unfortunately, agreement has been no more easily achieved by these investigators than by the content-analysis specialists. The reader should listen to the next person who engages him in conversation. How would the reader define an utterance? Is it all the words his conversational partner says until he stops and it is the reader's turn to speak? Or is it all the words in a part of a sentence that he utters fluently until he pauses for a breath so that hesitations for breathing define a logical place to end and begin a unit? But if he chooses the latter approach to "unitizing," how long will the pause have to be before it is really scored as a pause? For example, one second? Or one hundredth of a second? Lest the reader conclude that these are academic questions, let us hasten to point out that most if not all the results that will be presented below quite probably would be changed markedly if the unit of study were defined in a manner different than the one we will present shortly.

The problem of how to define an utterance length probably began with the work of Norwine and Murphy (1938), two specialists working for the Bell System. They monitored and analyzed 51 telephone calls between the Chicago and New York City business offices of the Bell System. The voice records were fed into a recording device that provided an oscillograph of the speech output of each of the two speakers in the 51 conversational pairs. Before proceeding with their analysis Norwine and Murphy had to define their speech measures. Their solution to the problem of what to record as a unit and how to record it is probably best presented in their own words.

> In the simplest case of conversational interchange each party speaks for a short time, pauses, and the other party replies. The time intervals are then simply the lengths of time each party speaks and the lengths of the pauses between speeches. The period during which there is speech may be called a talkspurt, and the length of the pause may be called the response time. These two quantities would then suffice to describe this simple type of interchange.
>
> In many instances, however, the process is not so orderly; for example, one speaker may pause and then resume speaking, or the listener may begin to reply without waiting for the end of the talker's speech. The possible, and indeed frequently encountered, variations of the simple cycle of which the preceding examples constitute only a fraction make it necessary to carefully define and delimit the elements into which a conversation may be resolved. It is believed that any telephonic conversation between two persons can be completely described in terms of the presence or absence of energy by the following time elements: "A *talkspurt* is speech by one party, including his pauses, which is preceded and followed, with or without intervening pauses, by speech from the other party perceptible to the one producing the talkspurt. Obvious exceptions to this definition are the initial and final talkspurts in a conversation. There may be simultaneous talkspurts by the two talkers; if one party is speaking and at the same time hears speech from the other, *double talking* is said to occur.
>
> *Resumption time* is the length of the pause intervening between two periods of speech within a talkspurt.
>
> *Response time* is the length of the interval between the beginning of a pause as heard by the listener and the beginning of his reply. It may be positive or negative. The pause to which reference is made

ordinarily occurs at the end of a talkspurt but may be a pause followed by a resumption of speech by the first talker (p. 282)."

From this description it is clear that for Norwine and Murphy, and their contemporary successors at the Bell Telephone Laboratories (see Brady, 1965, 1968, 1969), the basic unit of utterance (a talkspurt) is what a layman might define as an utterance, namely, *everything* said (or the total speaking duration consumed) by one person from the moment he begins a new speech unit to the time he signals to his conversational partner that he is through with his share of his contribution and thus that the latter may now speak.

DURATION OF UTTERANCE

Because all the research that will be reviewed later depends upon the reader's understanding what we recorded as a unit of utterance, an example of a total interview (employment) is given in the appendix of this volume (following the references). The job interview was conducted by one of the authors with an applicant for the position of patrolman in the same city. He was one of the 60 subjects in a second study we carried out on the relationship between the *content* of speech (what the interviewee is talking about) and the noncontent measures being studied by us (for example, how long he speaks per utterance about his *occupational* background versus his *educational* or *family* background). The Interviewer (Joseph D. Matarazzo) is designated as "I," while the applicant is shown as "A," in the transcription. Except for the necessary changes in or omissions of places and names of individuals that we made to protect the anonymity of our respondents, the interview transcription is not altered in any way. In all our research, and in the accompanying transcribed sample interview, *an utterance (or speech unit) is recorded as the total duration of time it takes a speaker to emit all the words he is contributing in that particular unit of exchange (as this would be judged by common social standards).*

In the transcribed interview in the Appendix single units of utterance for each speaker are transcribed next to his identifying designation ("I" or "A"). Thus, for example, as shown in the transcription, the interviewer's first (single) utterance includes three sentences: "How do you do, Mr. ______? My name is Dr. ______. Can you tell me how you happened to apply for a patrolman's position with the city of ______?" Conversely, even though the interviewer's second utterance (beginning with "You say . . . ," and ending with ". . . to you") constitutes two sentences, it still is recorded as a single utterance. Likewise, the applicant's first single utterance is defined as everything he said between "Well" and the words ". . . sounded real interesting to me." It should be clear that an utterance can contain only one word (such as "Yes" or "Why?"), or two words (for example, the applicant's response "My dad?" in the middle of the appended interview), or it can contain many hundreds of words. In addition, an incomplete utterance—but nevertheless recorded as a full utterance—can terminate in the middle of a sentence as, for example, when the other person interrupts and the first speaker clearly stops speaking (either for a clearly defined pause or until the interrupting partner completes the utterance which constituted the interruption). In our studies, and following Norwine and Murphy and the anthropologist Eliot D. Chapple (1942) whose speech research gave impetus to our own investigations, we have defined a speech unit as an utterance separated at either end by two silence periods—one silence following the other participant's last comment (that is, the speaker's *latency* or response time) and the second silence following the speaker's own comment and preceding the listener's next comment (that is, the listener's latency).[1] Pauses for breathing, for choosing words, for reflection, for stuttering and stammering or other hesitation phenomena, or related disfluencies (what Norwine and Murphy call "resumption time") do *not* signal the end of that particular utterance. Rather, they are included in the definition and record-

1. A schematic diagram of the units of measurement we have utilized in our speech research is provided in Figure 5.3 and should enhance the reader's understanding of our measures. Interrelationships among some of these variables are discussed later by us and also in an excellent book by Jaffe and Feldstein (1970). Comparison of the latter's Figure II–2 (1970, p. 20) with our Figure 5.3 will make clear the similarities and differences in definitions of the speech measures in both research programs.

ing of a single utterance when the *content* clearly suggests (and both conversational partners clearly appear to acknowledge) that, despite this disfluency, the current speaker has not completed that utterance. An example of one utterance or unit is: "Yes, I can tell you about . . . (pause) . . . my father. He was a . . . (pause) . . . how can I say it . . . (pause) . . . a man of many talents. You would . . . (pause) . . . have . . . (pause) . . . liked him." However, pauses (again determined by context) that precede the introduction of new ideas or thoughts by the same individual, *without an intervening comment by the other interview participant,* signal the onset of a *new* speech unit. For example: "It's true that I've . . . (pause) . . . enjoyed hunting for most of my life." (Pause two to three seconds) . . . "Speaking of hunting, I'm reminded of a favorite dog I had several years ago." The context clearly suggested that one unit ended with "life" and a second, or new unit, began with "Speaking." See Rogers (1942, pp. 265–437) and Wolberg (1954, pp. 688–780) for numerous examples of typical single interview units as scored by us. We have found observer reliability for this duration of utterance variable and the other variables here described (reaction time latency, initiative time latency, and number and percentage of interruptions) to be unusually high (Phillips, Matarazzo, Matarazzo, and Saslow, 1957; Wiens, Molde, Holman, and Matarazzo, 1966). Other investigators have confirmed the finding of high observer (or inter-scorer) reliability of one or another of these four speech variables (Chapple, 1949, p. 301; Goldman-Eisler, 1951, p. 355; Cervin, 1956, p. 164; Mahl, 1956a, p. 4; Kanfer and Marston, 1962, p. 427; Siegman and Pope, 1965, pp. 525–526; Pope and Siegman, 1966, p. 150; and Jaffe and Feldstein, 1970, p. 132).

Beginning in 1939 Chapple used essentially this common sense definition of a unit of interaction to characterize human relationships, and he studied the frequency and duration of such alternating series of what he called actions and inactions in a variety of two-person pairs or dyads (supervisor–supervisee; personnel interviewer–job applicant; doctor–patient). A summary of this work is given in Chapple (1949). Although he included in his unit of communicative action (our duration of utterance variable) all *verbal* as well as *nonverbal* communications (for example, talking, smiling, head nodding), and we earlier followed this practice, we soon came to learn that, relative to verbal exchanges and with the exceptions of highly unique situations such as some segments of psychotherapy or those reviewed by Jaffe and Feldstein (1970, p. 13), the occurrence of smiling, head nodding, and other forms of nonverbal communicative gestures *in isolation* (without concurrent speech) rarely constitute more than a very small fraction of any sample of conversation. Consequently, these nonverbal gestures can be *omitted* from the definition of a unit of utterance with little or no loss in fidelity (Wiens, Molde, Holman, and Matarazzo, 1966). This latter is what we have done for approximately the past ten years.[2]

To obtain an average (mean) of a speaker's duration of utterance in any single conversation one adds up all the individual, or single, durations of utterance he emitted and divides this sum of durations by their total number of occurrences (mean duration of A's utterance equals the sum of all A's single utterances divided by the total number of such single units of utterance emitted by A. The same procedure is followed for speaker B).

In common with Norwine and Murphy, we also have recorded and studied three additional first-order speech measures: *interruptions* (what they call two *simultaneous talkspurts,* or double talking), *reaction time latency* (their response time), and *initiative time latency* (elapsed time separating any two bona fide

2. However, although we learned in the Wiens et al. (1966) study that our duration of utterance variable—even then being defined by us as vocal behavior alone and *excluding* all gestures and other nonvocal communicative behavior, is, for all practical purposes, synonymous with a definition of utterance duration that does include such nonvocal communication—there obviously are some studies in which an investigator will by design elect to investigate such nonverbal behavior, per se, or in combination with vocal utterance length. Nevertheless, the beginning researcher in this area will learn from the Wiens et al. study that our duration of utterance variable yields the *identical* measure whether recorded from the "live" interview itself or from a tape recording of the same interview or both, or whether recorded in either manner by an experienced or a totally inexperienced observer.

complete single utterances, in our terminology, or talkspurts in Norwine and Murphy's, emitted by the *same* speaker without an intervening utterance by his partner).

INTERRUPTION

An interruption is defined as any instance of simultaneous speech by two (or more) speakers. Its frequency is merely the number of times it occurs, whereas its duration is the length of time overlap occurs in each instance of interrupting speech. Percentage interruption for each speaker is merely the total number of times he spoke in a conversation divided into the number of these same speech units (frequency) that were interruptions of his partner (for example, number of times A interrupted his partner divided by total number of times A spoke in that same conversation; the same for speaker B).

REACTION TIME LATENCY

A reaction time latency is the *duration of silence* separating one speaker's just completed utterance from his partner's next succeeding utterance, that is, the duration of time from the moment one person in the dyad terminates an utterance until the second person begins his next comment. Thus latency silence is merely a measure of the reaction time variable so well known in psychology. In the interview transcribed in the appendix of this book reaction time latencies begin at the end of each speaker's completed utterance and end when the other person begins. To obtain an average (mean) of a speaker's reaction time in any single conversation, one adds up all the individual reaction time latencies and divides this sum of durations by their total number of occurrences (frequency).

INITIATIVE TIME LATENCY

Another type of silence duration occurs in interviews or other dyadic (or multi-person) conversations when the second person (often the interviewer in professional settings), or another member of the conversational group, does *not* respond following the termination of the first person's (the interviewee's) last unit of speech. Interviewers typically do not respond to each completed utterance given by an interviewee. Rather, even though it clearly appears to be their turn to speak, they will remain silent to permit the interviewee to speak again even though he has contributed the last comment. While occurring less frequently in larger group settings, it occasionally happens that no member will respond to the last speaker, and he "initiates" another utterance himself. While reaction time (or latency) as a variable, would appear to be an appropriate term for the case where the interviewee responds to an utterance just contributed by the interviewer (or vice versa), the same term would not appear to be appropriate to describe the silence duration in those instances where the person after a silence interval *himself* contributes another utterance (without an intervening utterance from his partner). We have used the term *initiative time latency* to describe the latter type of silence duration. A mean or average is computed for this variable for each speaker by summing all the individual initiative time latency durations he contributed and dividing this figure by their total number or frequency of occurrence. Percentage initiative time latency for each speaker is obtained by dividing the frequency (number) of initiative latency units he contributed by the total number of times (frequency) this same speaker spoke (total frequency of his single units of utterance) in the total conversational sample during which an interviewer has created conditions for initiative behavior to occur (for example, when the interviewer purposely waits five to ten seconds each time before answering the interviewee).

DEFINITIONS OF SPEECH UNITS USED BY OTHER INVESTIGATORS

Numerous other investigators have studied durations of utterances or hesitation phenomena. However, the majority of these workers have attempted to *circumvent* the necessity of using a human observer to make the necessary decisions as to when an utterance (or reaction or initiative time latency) begins and ends. They have had the two conversational partners who were being monitored each speak directly into a microphone attached to a recording device, which was programmed to electronically record beginnings and endings of each speech unit merely by registering the presence or absence of sound energy from one or both microphone units. Each momentary hesitation or other speech disfluency would be interpreted by the recording instrument as the end of a single unit of utterance. The next word emitted, ending the disfluency, would be interpreted by the automatic recording device as the beginning of a second or separate utterance. What our human observer would record as a single utterance of, for example, 32 seconds, might be recorded by such electronic devices as nine separate and different single units of utterances. Most workers since Verzeano and Finesinger (1949) have experimented with *arbitrarily* increasing or decreasing pause durations that could occur in a single ongoing utterance but still not be recorded by the instrument as two or more separate utterances. All these workers have found that the results obtained in their research are grossly affected by the arbitrary length of the speech disfluency (silence) tolerated by the recording instrument in the definition of a single unit of utterance.

Excellent discussions of the differing results obtained by such purely electronic, automatic, and nonhuman observers can be found in the papers by Verzeano (1950, 1951); Mahl (1956a, 1956b); Starkweather (1959, 1964); Hargreaves (1960); Hargreaves and Starkweather (1959); Cassotta, Feldstein, and Jaffe (1964); Siegman and Pope (1965); Ramsay (1966); Ramsay and Law (1966); and Brady (1965, 1968, 1969).

One British investigator, Frieda Goldman-Eisler, has pursued a very active program of study of hesitations, pauses, and other *intra-utterance* disfluencies (Norwine and Murphy's resumption times) that occur in interviews and other conversational speech. She has shown in a number of studies and in a summary volume (Goldman-Eisler, 1968) that most human speech, what we are here calling single utterances of the type transcribed in the interview in the Appendix, is made up of *short phrases* (a group of a few words) followed by hesitation or other disfluencies, followed by another short phrase, still another hesitation, and so on.

Her finding is sufficiently interesting that a typical sample of it (Goldman-Eisler, 1962, p. 38) has been adapted and is presented in Figure 1.1. The Figure shows that, in the representative sample of humans studied, each conversing in a number of different speaking situations but here lumped together in one figure, a

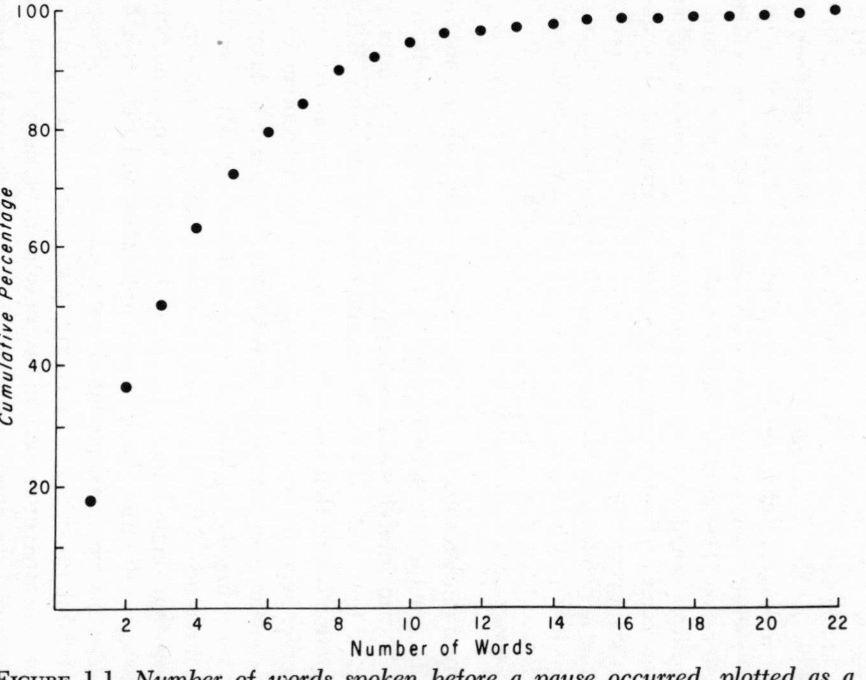

FIGURE 1.1. *Number of words spoken before a pause occurred, plotted as a cumulative frequency (percentage).*

pause (intra-utterance disfluency) occurred after only two spoken words in 36 percent of these single units of speech (single durations of utterances), and it occurred at least once after only six words in 80 percent, and after twelve words in 98 percent of such single verbal communicative units. Goldman-Eisler (1962, pp. 37–38) writes:

> The fact that springs to notice immediately on seeing these visual records is the discontinuous nature of speech. We rarely achieve a continuous flow of verbal output in spontaneous speech. In most cases our speech utterances are series of verbal productions of different lengths which are broken up into discrete elements by pauses of varying duration. Speech and pauses alternate in continuous succession. The length of pauses varies over a wide range and may reach the length of several seconds. Apart from their length, hesitation pauses turned out to be a remarkably frequent phenomenon. Indeed [as seen in Figure 1.1] more than half of our speech seems to issue in phrases of less than four words and [more than] three quarters in sequences of less than six words. Only a very small proportion of speech consists of sequences uttered in one flow of more than twelve words [that is, without an intervening disfluency].

She found results similar to those here reproduced in Figure 1.1 in spontaneous speech, practiced or rehearsed speech, and in psychiatric interviews. It is because humans rarely utter more than a few words of each communicative utterance before a hesitation occurs that, in our research, we have employed a human observer who utilizes the *context* (namely the content of what the speaker is saying) to decide whether to release or keep down the recording key which he depressed when the speaker began the utterance. Most investigators use electronic "observers" and report that single human utterances typically average one or two seconds in duration (see, for example, Jaffe and Feldstein, 1970, p. 22, who report an average vocalization length of 1.64 seconds in natural dialogues). In contrast, we have found that single communicative utterances in two person conversations (especially interviews) are considerably longer and often average between 20 and 40 seconds (see subsequent figures).

Nevertheless, pursuing her own important interests, Goldman-Eisler has discovered some interesting facts about intrautterance pauses. She has shown that such pauses or hesitations (1) are related to the degree of *information* carried by words or word segments (1958a, 1958b, 1961a); (2) are sometimes unfilled blank pauses and at other times are filled with hesitation phenomena such as "ah" (1961b); (3) decrease in frequency with several consecutive repetitions of the same speech task (1961c); (4) yield frequency distributions that vary in shape as a function of the type of situation in which the speech is uttered (1961d); (5) occur after only three words in 50 percent of spoken speech utterances and after 10 or fewer words in 90 percent of such single verbal communicative units (1961e; and our Figure 1.1); (6) occupy between 40 and 50 percent of the total communicative speech unit duration and reflect both an automatic mechanical, purely motor, or vocal process and very complex thought processes (1962); (7) are selectively affected in individual speakers by administration of the drug Chlorpromazine and less so by the drug Sodium Amytal (Goldman-Eisler, Skarbek and Henderson, 1965).

In his Yale University laboratory, Mahl (1956a, 1956b, 1959) has conducted an equally impressive program of research on intra-utterance disfluencies such as "ah" and related hesitations. He has studied especially their occurrence during the verbalization of emotional utterances of the type frequently occurring in psychotherapy.

The studies conducted by Goldman-Eisler and Mahl, although focusing on intra-utterance hesitation phenomena, provide an excellent example of what behavioral scientists can learn by creative and painstaking study of mundane phenomena such as spoken phrase lengths, verbal disfluencies, and related speech characteristics. On a more limited scale one might study, for example, (1) whether tape recorded conversations reveal a difference between liberal arts and engineering majors in the number of words spoken before an intra-utterance disfluency occurs; or (2) whether Presidents Lyndon B. Johnson or Richard M. Nixon have more or fewer such disfluencies than did the more seemingly articulate President John F. Kennedy (records of these speeches are easily purchased); or (3) whether the sales executive in his company has different speech characteristics from a comparable level executive from the production department; or (4) whether fewer disfluencies are present when a young man is on the first date or the twentieth date with the same girl, or (5) the effect of a course in public speaking on the speaker's own level of disfluencies.

Mechanical Aids to Data Gathering

Until recently, experienced investigators conducting such research needed little equipment except stop watches, ink-pen writers, or tape recorders. (Such research can still be conducted inexpensively as shown by Matarazzo, Holman, and Wiens, 1967.) Nevertheless, early pioneers such as Chapple quickly began a search for mechanical aids to data gathering. The most important of these he called the Interaction Chronograph.

THE CHAPPLE INTERACTION CHRONOGRAPH

A history of the development of various early forms of this instrument will be found in the paper by Chapple and Donald (1946), while a description and photograph of the more elaborate present instrument will be found in a subsequent publication by Chapple (1949).

Originally, Chapple used a simple stop watch as his instrument. With this, he or his observer recorded the duration of contacts between pairs of individuals (two individuals talking together or one handing the other a tool or some similar interaction) and recorded the results on paper ruled off in divisions for each minute that passed. He measured the length of each contact in minutes and also the length of time between contacts, and from these measurements he characterized interpersonal relationships in terms of *frequency* of contact, *average duration* of contact, *total time* spent together, and so on. He also recorded which of the two persons *initiated* the contact. These observations were made of interactions taking place in factories (both worker and executive interactions), in a department store, and in several political organizations.

To get more accurate observations and at the same time to reduce the burden of the observer, Chapple next developed a simple recording device consisting of a moving roll of paper driven at a uniform speed upon which individual ink-writing pens continuously drew lines when the individual speaker keys were pressed down. When an individual started to act, for example initiating a contact, the observer would depress the key assigned to that person. When he stopped acting, his key would be released and the line would end. The blank space between the inked lines provided a measure of his inactivity. The same procedure was used for each person under observation.

With this innovation, Chapple could measure not only the length of time each person talked (his action) and the length of time he was silent (silence variable), obtaining a continuous record of this sequence of action and silence, but he could also record variations in the verbal *adjustment* of the participants to each other. The record indicated who interrupted, how long the interruption lasted, and, for example, which one *dominated* by talking the other down. Further, if there was a silence during which one person failed to respond to the other, the record indicated who was responsible for the silence, how long the silence lasted (who was failing to "adjust" and how long this failure of adjustment lasted), and whether the first speaker finally *initiated* the next action.

Chapple could do more with his instrument than record these basic elements of the pattern of give-and-take in a conversation or psychiatric interview. If, for example, in an interview one person tended to dominate the interview, taking the greater portion of the time and, when interrupted, increasing the length of each speech to out-talk the other person, it could be determined with accuracy how the other person reacted. Did he tend to become more silent as the other talked more and more, or, refusing to become completely dominated, did he increase his own activity and try to hold his own? Measurements could also be made of his degree of adjustment to the person who was doing most of the talking. Did he interrupt or fail to respond, and if so, how frequently and for what duration?

These data and cumulative curves drawn from them were arrived at only after laborious measurement (human) by ruler of the ink-drawn lines recorded on the moving tape. To reduce the tedium of the measurements, Chapple next developed a computer, the Interaction Chronograph, that would draw cumulative curves of the interaction patterns while these were being recorded by the observer; that is, much as Skinner's animals have always plotted their own learning curves. When the interview ended, a series of graphs had been drawn on a wide sheet of paper and, by the use of a plexiglass scale, complete measurements of the desired variables (for example, the durations, the slopes or rates of activity) could be obtained from these graphs.

Though used by Chapple for personnel selection and research in industry for several years, this model was limited in several ways: it did not give measurements of all the variables thought useful for even one person, and it was not designed to yield completely independent values for the interviewer. Moreover, it seemed to Chapple that, since the final step in scoring was to obtain numerical values for the observed interaction, it would be desirable to develop a machine that, in addition to recording the interaction of both persons completely, converted the raw measurements directly into the desired numerical data. Graphs would be eliminated; scoring time would be reduced immensely; the obtained scores would be less vulnerable to scorer-errors.

The new model of the Interaction Chronograph, a photograph of which was published in 1949 (Chapple, 1949), was the instrument we used in our own research program from 1954 through about 1961. It consisted of two parts: a small observer's box and a large recording machine with which the former is connected by a long flexible cable, providing for the possibility of the two parts being housed in different rooms.

The observer's box had five keys or buttons operated manually by the observer while the interview was in progress. Two of these buttons controlled the power and turned the larger recording machine on and off. A third button was a signal marker that activated a designated electrical counter in the recording machine. The purpose of this signal counter was to enable the observer to mark the introduction of a change at a particular point during the interview. The two remaining keys were designated, one each, for the interviewer and interviewee. After turning on the two power keys and pushing the signal button to indicate the start of a new observation, the observer had only to keep one finger on the interviewer's key and one finger on his other hand on the subject's key to record the subsequent interaction. Each time the designated person started to talk (and for Chapple, nodding the head, gesturing, or communicating in any other form), the observer pressed his key and kept it down, releasing the key only when the action came to an end. The observer's task was to press a key when an utterance began, record how long it continued (key down), and when it terminated (key released). Since this kind of record was kept for both persons simultaneously in the situation, a complete and chronological record of their interaction was available.

The Interaction Chronograph, which recorded these two-person interactions, was nothing more than a very elaborate electrical stop watch that recorded time-based events as they occurred. The tedious computations that had to be made by the observer when Chapple was using only a stop watch or pen ink-writer were now all computed electrically and simultaneously simply as a function of the combinations possible from an analysis of the positions of the two keys—interviewer and interviewee—relative to each other. However, the interaction record produced by the Interaction Chronograph still required a scorer who would have to sum arithmetically and by hand the various machine inputs to obtain an utterance-by-utterance record of the verbal interaction.

THE INTERACTION RECORDER

The printed record produced by the Chapple Interaction Chronograph could later be scored to produce *mean* scores on 12 different measures. However, only three of these measures—units, tempo, activity—were primary or first-order variables. The remaining nine measures were second-order or derivative variables. Measures of two major variables—speech and silence—which have been shown by us (Matarazzo, Saslow, and Hare, 1958) to account for about 88 percent of the variance of the 12 measures, could not be read directly from the Chapple Interaction Chronograph, although they could be derived fairly readily by a scorer. While it was possible, from the printed Interaction Chronograph records, to obtain sums of raw scores, the record did not permit calculation of the variance of any of these variables. To meet these needs, Chapple devised a scoring scheme that yielded a *unit-by-unit* record of interviewer and interviewee speech, silence, and interruptions through simple calculation from his complex measures. However, scoring a chronograph record in this way, while highly reliable, was a tedious chore.

To permit faster processing of data, we collaborated with the University of Oregon Medical School Research Instrument Service in automating the scoring of interview speech and silence interactions. Specifically, we wished to record more efficiently on punched paper tape a record of the sequences of interview speech and silence: a record of when one or the other, both, or neither person was speaking. It was necessary that the equipment translate our time readings into a binary code acceptable to a Burroughs E101 computer, which we had purchased for this purpose.

The new Interaction Recorder consists of a commercial timer (Computer Measurements Corporation), a commercial punch unit (Tally), and other circuitry designed by our Research Instrument Service (for technical details see Johnston, Jansen, Weitman, Hess, Matarazzo, and Saslow, 1961). The CMC timer, which provides the time base for our system, has a binary coded decimal output that was converted to a 1-2-4-8 code acceptable to our computer. The tape perforator is a Tally Model 420, which is capable of punching up to 60 digits per second. It generates tape words consisting of eight digits of information: (1) begin word, a standard symbol for the computer; (2) period signal, denoting the end of a section of the interview; (3) identification, who is speaking; (4, 5, 6, 7) four digits of time; and (8) end word, another standard symbol for the computer. The tape is read by a Burroughs E101 or an IBM 1100 series computer, which have been programmed to produce a printed chronological unit-by-unit analysis of the speech, silence, and interruptions as they occur sequentially throughout the interview.

Except that the Chapple Interaction Chronograph records time in one-hundredths of a minute while the Interaction Recorder uses seconds as its unit of time, the comparability of data recording by these two devices was found to be nearly identical (Wiens, Matarazzo, and Saslow, 1965).[3] To record the interview interaction with the Interaction Recorder, a trained observer is still needed who can see and hear the interview behind a one-way mirror and record each unit of speech by activating either the interviewer or interviewee "key." At the beginning of either participant's speech unit the appropriate key is depressed (or both, when both participants are talking simultaneously), and at the completion of that speech unit the key is released. The observer's task is essentially identical when recording on either of the two devices.

THE MULTIPLE INTERACTION RECORDER

In the past several years we have improved upon the interaction recorder and have developed a *Multiple Interaction Recorder* (Morris, Johnston, Bailey, and Wiens, 1968), which has two improvements over the Interaction Recorder. It contains 20 speaker keys, thereby permitting us to record groups of speakers numbering up to twenty individuals. Whereas the Interaction Recorder uses punched paper tape, the Multiple Interaction Recorder uses a highly efficient, incremental magnetic tape unit that is also later fed into an IBM computer for almost instantaneous scoring of hours of recorded interaction.

The cost of initial development and the cost of annual operation of sophisticated recording devices such as our Interaction Recorder and Multiple Interaction Recorder or the Automatic Vocal Transaction Analyzer designed by Cassotta, Feldstein, and Jaffe (1964), or devices like the Duration Tabulator developed by Hargreaves and Starkweather (1959), run into many thousands of dollars. Some of the same speech variables we and other groups of investigators have studied can be investigated using only a tape recorder and stop watch (Matarazzo, Holman, and Wiens,

3. *Initiative time latency,* which we discuss in numerous places throughout this book could not be recorded and abstracted efficiently with the Chapple Interaction Chronograph, but it could be done with the new Interaction Recorder. Thus, some of the studies reported here will include this variable and others will not.

1967). For example, we have shown that a mere "word count," the number of words in each spoken utterance, is an exact substitute measure (correlation of .98) of the duration of that utterance in seconds as recorded by the Interaction Recorder or similar expensive recording device. Mahl (1959, p. 115) and Siegman, Pope, and Blass (1969, p. 542) similarly report correlations of .91 and .92, respectively, between duration of utterance in seconds and number of words in the same utterance. Simple measures such as "word count" became feasible following our study that showed that analyzing verbal interactions from a tape recording is about as reliable as recording the same interaction "live" (Wiens, Molde, Holman, and Matarazzo, 1966). Lauver (1970) has recently described a method of constructing a Chapple Interaction Chronograph from the motor of a backyard barbecue grill and other inexpensive accessories.

The Accuracy of the Observer

These simple measures notwithstanding, it will be apparent from the earlier discussion that the observer (or "listener–observer" in recording from tape recordings) is an important person in the conduct of research since he is, in effect, part of the recording instrument. He records and, therefore, contributes all data. He must be a faithful transmitter of the interviewer–interviewee (or other conversational group's) verbal behavior. It is important that he go through a practice series of recording some five to ten interviews or conversations before beginning an investigative enterprise using sophisticated equipment. (If the reader were employing "word count" from a tape recording of the conversation as his measure, he can achieve a high level of accuracy by merely replaying each tape segment until he is certain of the accuracy of his word count data.)

Because we felt early in our research program that it was necessary to check the reliability (accuracy) of human observers, we conducted a study in which two observers simultaneously recorded the two-person interaction occurring in job interviews. One observer recorded from one side of a room, while the second observer made similar, but completely independent, observations from the other side of the same room. The results revealed that the level of agreement in their two interaction recordings of 17 employment interviews was essentially 100 percent (Phillips, Matarazzo, Matarazzo, and Saslow, 1957). We therefore concluded that agreement between observers as to when an utterance (or reaction time latency, etc.) begins and ends is high enough to insure the comparability of data collected by any minimally practiced observers. The Wiens, Molde, Holman, and Matarazzo (1966) study, mentioned above, which successfully compared an observer who scored interviews "live" (while they were actually going on) against observers who later scored the same interaction from a tape recording also attests to the accuracy level of such observers. Jaffe and Feldstein (1970, p. 132) and Conger (1971, p. 56) have independently confirmed the very high inter-observer or inter-rater reliability values reported in the earlier Phillips et al. (1957) and the Wiens, Molde, Holman, and Matarazzo (1966) study.

From time to time we have been asked by other investigators whether, for example as happens in many of the interview scoring systems reviewed by Kiesler (1972), our observer utilizes "the preceding or succeeding utterances" or other "contextual cues" to decide when a person's utterance has ended. Such questions imply a greater complexity to our duration of utterance variable than is actually involved, as a few minutes of experience with our system demonstrates. Our duration of utterance variable is merely what the man in the street would record if he were asked to press a button when a person began to speak to his conversational partner and to release it when *that* conversational unit ended. We provide dozens upon dozens of such examples of single units of utterance in the verbatim interview in the Appendix to this volume. Additionally, the Wiens et al. (1966) study empirically demonstrated that an interview can be reliably recorded on merely the first trial ("cold") by a completely *inexperienced* observer who merely is provided the simple definition of a duration of utterance presented above—simple because it accords with millions of such decisions he has made in judging such utterance endings in his own conversational lifetime—and given a tape recording of an interview to score. He turns on the tape recorder and can record the durations of utterance of both participants with unusual fidelity (reliability) on his first listening.

Investigators using our variables also question the possible length of the interview segment. For example, must an investigator score a whole 50-minute interview by our variables or can he sample segments of it, perhaps 5- or 15-minute durations and still get reliable and valid results? Our own experience (Matarazzo, 1962, pp. 497–499) and that of Tuason et al. (1961) and others clearly indicates that a 10- or 15-minute sample of an hour's interview is a fairly reliable measure of our speech measures from the same full hour. Correlations of such a segment with the whole hour are of the order of .80. However, there are undoubtedly emotional or other affective exchanges that occur in a few minutes' segment that clearly are *not* representative of the whole hour. One example is a 5-minute single communication about a despised parent emitted by an interviewee otherwise speaking in utterance lengths averaging 22 seconds. For this reason we discourage the use of our variables with interview segments shorter than 10 to 15 minutes in length. Additionally, we are also asked occasionally whether one whole interview is representative of, for example, a total therapy exchange that occurred over 70 such single interviews. The results discussed in Chapter 3 will reveal that a 50-minute interview is a reliable sample of a person's interview speech behavior when judged against a second, or retest interview. However, actual sequential psychotherapy interview data of the type shown here in Figure 4.11 and detailed in full for all our variables in Matarazzo et al. (1968) leaves no question that our interview variables can and do change as they mirror changes in, for example, the emotional (and content) exchanges that take place in psychotherapy.

2

The Anatomy of Speech Behavior

For a society that has extensively studied so many other facets of human behavior it may come as a surprise that we know so little about speaking behavior, an activity in which everyone probably engages in dozens of times daily. Recently increased interest among behavioral scientists in verbal behavior should enlarge our understanding of the nature of such communicative activity.

Frequency Distribution of Durations of Single Units of Utterance

The very essence of human conversation—its content—is carried by acoustical events that constitute durations of communicative utterances. More than thirty years ago Norwine and Murphy (1938, p. 288) tabulated and plotted the lengths (durations) of the 2,845 individual utterances (talkspurts) that occurred in the 51 business long distance telephone conversations they analyzed. Since then many other investigators have plotted frequency distributions of such single utterances in order to discern the characteristics of the frequency of occurrence of speech units of different lengths (Chapple, 1940; Verzeano, 1950, 1951; Saslow, Matarazzo, and Guze, 1955; Starkweather, 1959; Hargreaves, 1960; Matarazzo, Hess, and Saslow, 1962; Matarazzo, 1965; Matarazzo, Wiens, and Saslow, 1965; Matarazzo, Wiens, Matarazzo, and Saslow, 1968; Brady, 1965, 1968, 1969; and Jaffe and Feldstein, 1970). All these investigators report the same finding—namely, that by far the largest percentage of such single units of communicative utterances are of short durations and that very few ever reach lengths exceeding 50 to 60 seconds. The plotted frequency distribution of their durations resemble the letter "L" or, in more formal language, take the form of an exponential decay function.

SPEECH DURATIONS OF JOB APPLICANTS AND A PSYCHOTHERAPY PATIENT

An example of such a distribution is shown in Figure 2.1. The data were obtained by an observer who recorded through a one-way mirror the twenty separate job interviews conducted by JDM with 20 applicants and the 12 consecutive psychotherapeutic interviews of a therapist (JDM) and a 21-year-old female patient (CD). The data from these psychotherapy interviews will be used to describe the distributions shown in Figure 2.1. During the 12 approximately 50-minute interviews the patient (CD) contributed 951 single utterances, while the psychotherapist contributed 909. When frequencies are plotted for different utterance durations, it is evident from Figure 2.1 that most of the individual speech units were under 30 seconds. For ease of visual interpretation these same data are plotted again as cumulative percentages in Figure 2.2. In this figure each dot (black for CD, white for JDM) represents six seconds. Forty-three percent of CD's single utterances during the whole of the 12 sessions were six seconds or less in duration; 54 percent were 12 seconds or shorter; 62 percent were 18 seconds or less; 90 percent were less than 66 seconds; 98 percent were less than 120 seconds. In the total of 951 utterances in the 12 sessions, her longest single utterance was 611 seconds, or slightly longer than 10 minutes. Figure 2.2 also shows that her average (mean) utterance was 25.5 seconds long; while her median[1] length of speech was 9.0 seconds.

1. The *median* is that value above and below which 50 percent of all the single observations lie. When data are skewed, or nonsymmetrical in their distribution, the median is a more representative index than is the (arithmetic) mean. The latter is heavily influenced by one or more extreme scores. *Sigma* is the standard deviation, a measure of the variability of the individual observations around the mean of each distribution.

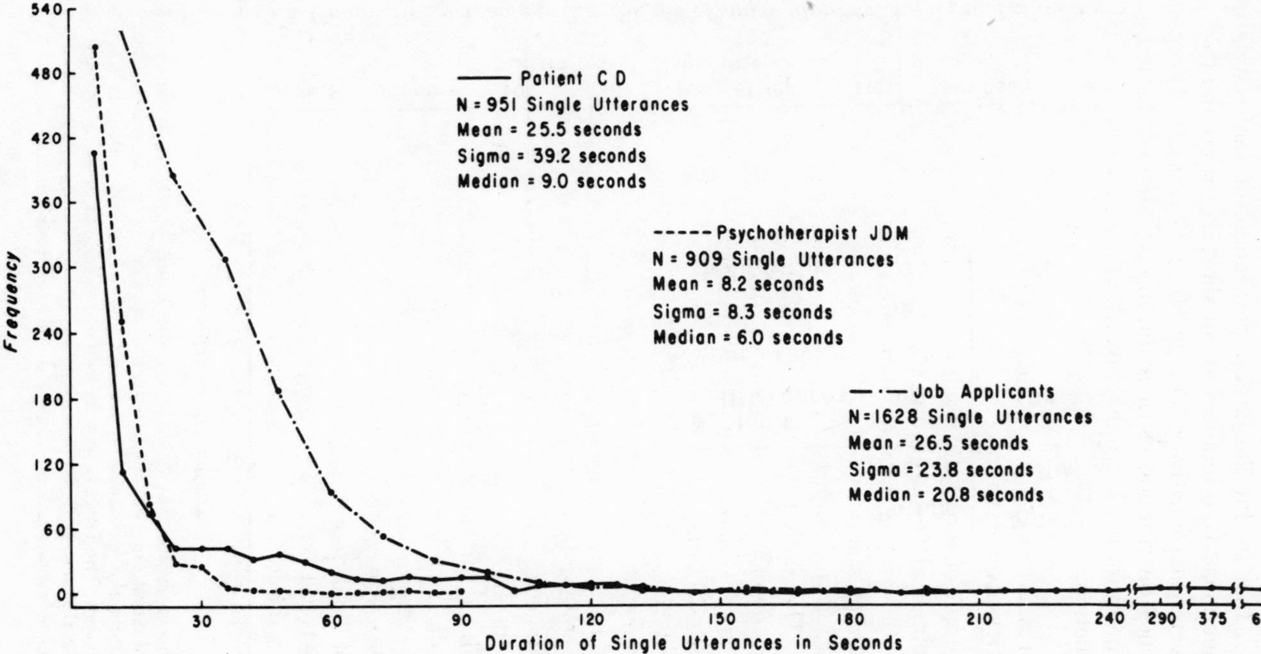

FIGURE 2.1. *Frequency distribution of single utterances of a psychotherapy patient, a psychotherapist, and 20 job applicants.*

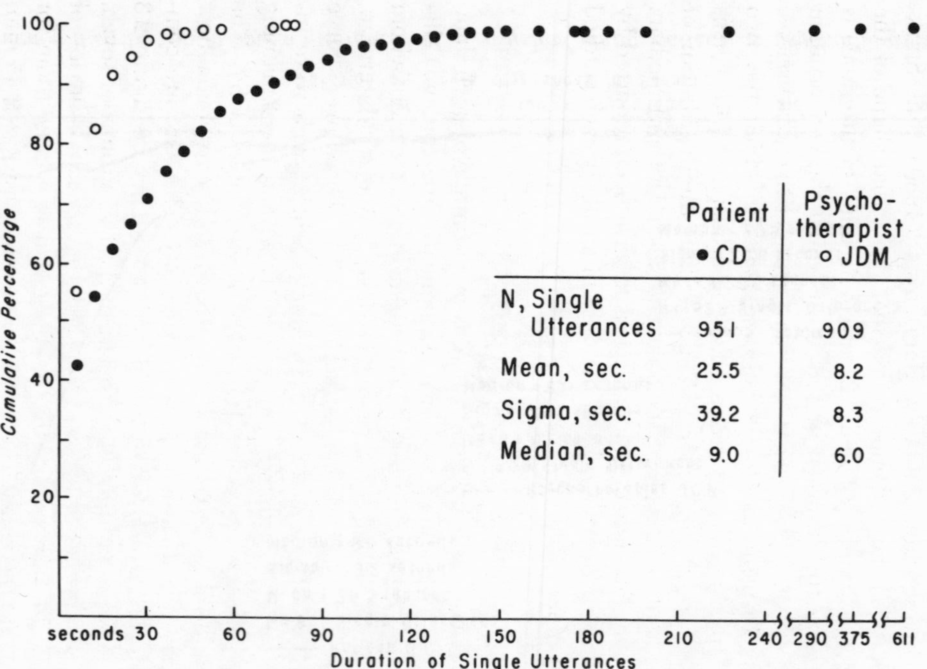

FIGURE 2.2. *Cumulative percentage distribution of single utterances of a psychotherapy patient, and a psychotherapist.*

The therapist speech durations reveal similar curves, although it is clear from Figure 2.2 that his individual speaking durations were considerably shorter than those of his patient; 92 percent of his utterances being 18 seconds or less in duration (in contrast to only 62 percent for the patient).

Other investigators, notably Hargreaves (1960) and Starkweather (1959), have demonstrated that the actual shape of the distribution (Figures 2.1 and 2.2) of single units of utterance is influenced by the situation or setting in which the conversation is taking place. Thus free discussions, competitive discussions, interviews focusing on life history, sessions in which the two speakers are role playing preassigned roles, husband-wife versus four-person conversations, and so on, all affect the distribution of utterance lengths as well as the values of the mean and median. However, to date actual data on this issue have been reported by investigators on only very small numbers of speakers each studied in two or more situations or settings.

SPEECH DURATIONS IN TWO DIFFERENT SETTINGS

Figure 2.3, not previously published, is one example of such data. It contains the frequency (shown as cumulative percentage) distribution of single units of speech of 14 nursing supervisors whom we had interviewed for a previous study (Wiens, Matarazzo, Saslow, Thompson, and Matarazzo, 1965). The lower curve shows the speech behavior of these nurses when seven were interviewed, one at a time, by one of us (JDM) and the remaining seven were interviewed by a psychiatrist-colleague (GS). The interviews averaged 35 minutes in length and focused on how each supervisor spent a typical working day. The data are combined into one group of 14 two-person interviews in Figure 2.3 since there were no differences between the two groups of seven. As part of another study we recorded the speech behavior of these same 14 nurses when they met together in a large room for weekly group meetings. These weekly meetings averaged 45 minutes in length and typically took as their focus a free and full verbal participation by the supervisors on a variety of nursing administration matters. Data for the first five such group meetings were averaged and are shown in the upper curve in Figure 2.3.

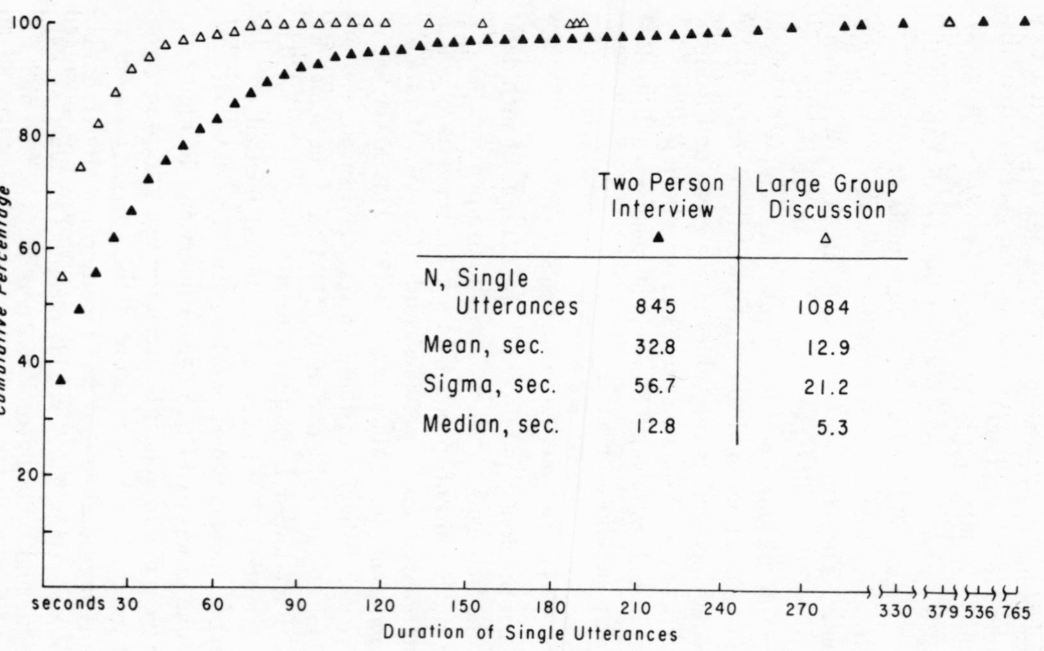

FIGURE 2.3. *Cumulative percentage distribution of single utterances of supervising nurses in a two-person interview and in discussion among themselves in a large group.*

The contrasting results clearly show the combined effect of at least two variables on speech behavior: *size* of conversational group (2-person versus 14-person) and *content* plus *setting* and *role expectancy* (how each spent a typical day, as related to a somewhat prestigious colleague–interviewer, versus free discussion of administrative matters with 13 supervisor–colleagues). The nurses spoke in utterances with a mean length of 32.8 seconds in the nondirective two-person interview; but they spoke in utterances lasting only an average (mean) of 12.9 seconds in the large-group meetings. Their mean unit of communicative speech was about one-third as long in the group situation (while talking with their peers) relative to the smaller two-person interview situation (in which they were talking to a person of presumed higher status in the hospital hierarchy). In the group setting 75 percent of the utterances were 12 seconds or less; in the two-person interview 75 percent were 42 seconds or less. While such instances were clearly exceptional and unrepresentative, the longest single utterance emitted in the five group meetings was 379 seconds (6.3 minutes), whereas its counterpart in the two-person interview was 765 seconds (12.7 minutes). If plotted as a frequency (raw) distribution comparable to the data shown in Figure 2.1, the cumulative percentage data shown in Figure 2.3 for both situations also would take the shape of an L. The incidental finding described above, that nurses talked in longer utterances with a high-status interviewer than they did when talking with their peers, is consistent with a finding reported by Siegman, Pope, and Blass (1969), that their female nursing students similarly talked more per utterance with a high-status interviewer than did the same individual nursing students with a lower-status interviewer. However, other variables also were operating.

SPEECH DURATIONS: INFLUENCE OF DIFFERENT INTERVIEWER SPEECH DURATIONS

In a study described in Chapter 4, the interviewer was instructed or "programmed" beforehand to speak in approximately 5-second utterances each time he spoke in one 15-minute segment of an interview and to speak in 10-second utterances in a second part of the same interview. The study was carried out as one part of a psychological assessment of 20 young patrolman applicants. As seen in Figure 2.4 the raw frequency distribution of the 20 applicants' single units of utterance again take an L shape, and this finding is independent of the length (5 seconds versus 10 seconds) of the individual speech units of the second conversational partner (the interviewer). The resulting larger mean applicant utterance length that can be discerned in Figure 2.4 when the interviewer himself spoke in longer utterances (10 seconds versus 5 seconds) will be discussed in a later section (Figure 4.2). Examples of other published L-shaped frequency (raw) distributions, in contrast to the cumulative percentages for comparable duration of utterance units, as well as other samples of distributions of single units of reaction time latencies similar to those presented in Figure 2.5 below, can be found in Matarazzo (1965, pp. 438–439), Matarazzo, Wiens, and Saslow (1965, pp. 184–185), and Jaffe and Feldstein (1970, pp. 69–77).

Frequency Distributions of Durations of Single Reaction Time Latencies

If one makes up a frequency distribution of the individual *reaction time latencies* occurring between the end of one speaker's utterance and the beginning of the second person's next remark, such a distribution of silence durations also takes the shape of an exponential decay function, or L, or, as some writers call it, a mirror-imaged J shape. Chapple (1939, p. 60; 1940, p. 12) was one of the first to report such J-shaped distributions, and his finding was followed by similar reports by Goldman-Eisler (1951, p. 357; 1961d, pp. 233–234); Saslow, Matarazzo, and Guze (1955, p. 424); Matarazzo, Hess, and Saslow (1962); Matarazzo (1965, pp. 438–439); Matarazzo, Wiens, and Saslow (1965, pp. 183–188); and Jaffe and Feldstein (1970, pp. 69–77; p. 110).

REACTION TIME LATENCIES OF JOB APPLICANTS AND A PSYCHOTHERAPY PATIENT

A typical example of such a distribution of the (raw) frequencies of such single reaction time latencies recently was published by Matarazzo, Wiens, Matarazzo, and Saslow (1968) and is repro-

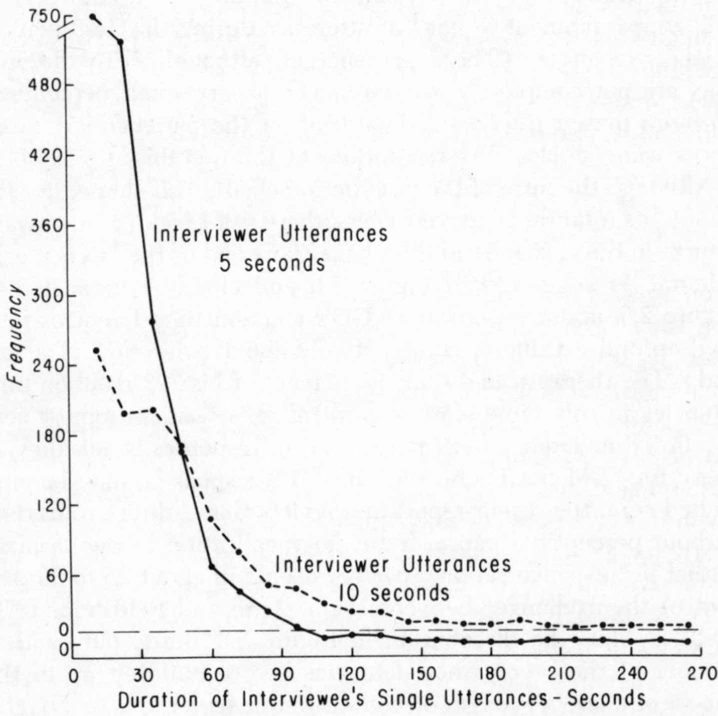

FIGURE 2.4. *Frequency distribution of single utterances of 20 job applicants.*

duced here in Figure 2.5. Part of the data were obtained in the recording of the same 12 psychotherapy interviews between JDM and CD that provided the data for the analysis of durations of utterance shown in Figures 2.1 and 2.2.

Although during the whole of the 12 sessions the patient–interviewee spoke 951 times, the interviewer responded to no more than 793 of these (see Figure 2.5). That is, at the completion of some 793 (83.4 percent) of the 951 patient utterances the therapist responded. He therefore failed to respond in some 158 (16.6 percent) of such utterance terminations, thereby creating an opportunity for the patient to "initiate" with another, or follow-up, comment to her last utterance during this 16.6 percent of the exchanges. (These percentages, although fairly descriptive, are not completely accurate since a very small percentage, no more than a fraction of 1 percent, of the patient's 951 utterances were "enclosed" interruptions of the therapist.)

Although the form of the distribution clearly is L shaped for the bulk of its total range, nevertheless, there is a break (a downward plunge in the L shape) in this at the short end of the latency continuum. As suggested in Figure 2.5 and clearly represented in Figure 2.6, about 8 percent of CD's reaction time latencies hovered around a value of zero (actually about two-tenths of a second). The therapist had some 27 percent of his 793 reaction time latencies in this same close-to-zero range. (That an almost zero reaction time latency in 27 percent of his responses is not idiosyncratic for JDM but is also typical of other speakers may be concluded from the recent report and review that a direct transition, without perceptible pause, from the vocalization of one speaker to that of his conversational partner occurs in about 25 to 26 percent of the exchanges between them [Jaffe and Feldstein, 1970, p. 10].) Thus the distribution in Figure 2.5 "starts out" with a number of these very short latencies before building up to the one-second latency length of *highest frequency* (the actual beginning of the L shape in the visual representation of the over-all distribution). From the value of one second shown in the raw frequencies in Figure 2.5, the distribution of the remaining frequencies steadily decreases to form the "vertical" and "tail" portions of the L shape.

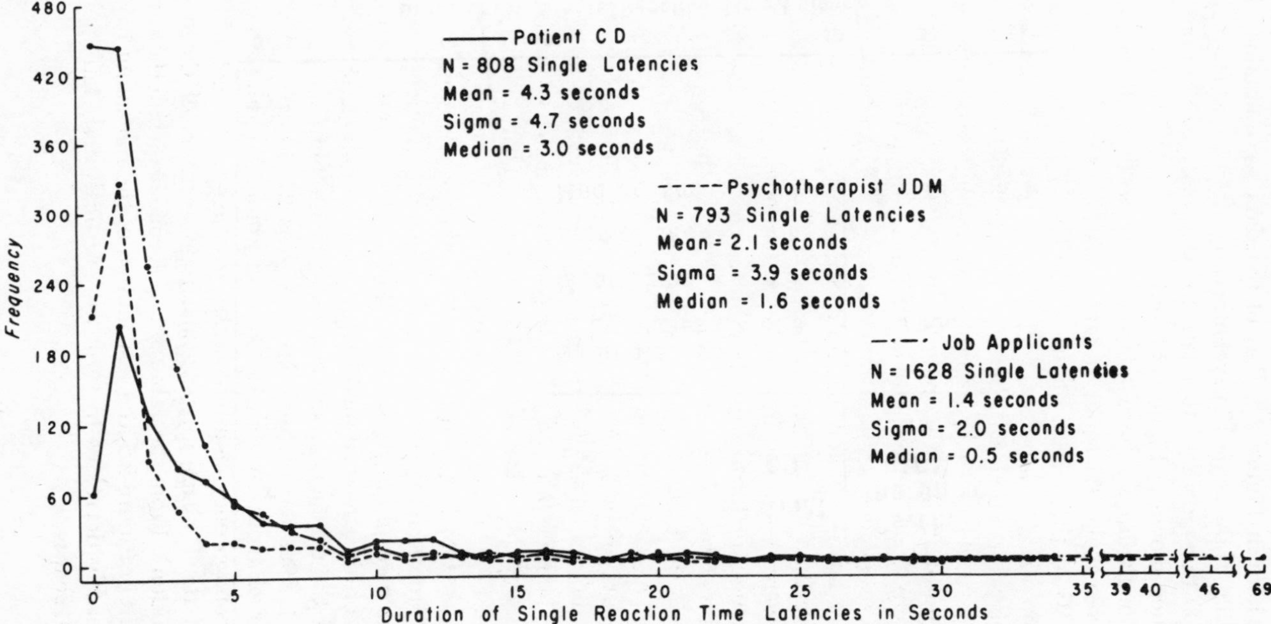

FIGURE 2.5. *Frequency distribution of single reaction time latencies of a psychotherapy patient, a psychotherapist, and 20 job applicants.*

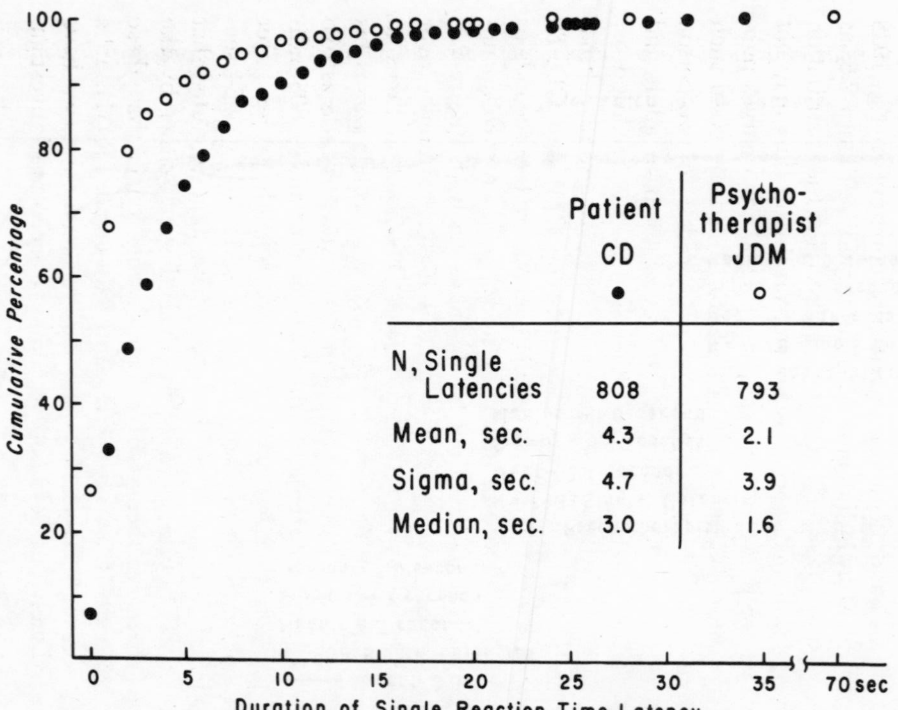

FIGURE 2.6. *Cumulative percentage distribution of single reaction time latencies of a psychotherapy patient and a psychotherapist.*

Norwine and Murphy (1938, pp. 288–289) first presented frequency distributions of utterances and reaction time latencies that visually revealed the presence of this "start effect" for both utterance and latency distributions, although it appears that Hargreaves (1960, p. 166) may have been the investigator who first named the phenomenon he observed in his *utterance*[2] distribution curves the "start effect." Following this lead we probably should refer to the similar phenomenon visually apparent in the 1938 Norwine and Murphy latency distribution and in Figure 2.5, as a *latency* "start effect." That the start effect for the distribution of latencies in human speech is not universal, and thus may *not* appear in some conversational samples, is clear from curves published by Goldman-Eisler (1961d, p. 234). Her data reveal such a start effect in the verbal interaction recorded in two-person psychiatric interviews, but failed to reveal them in adult and adolescent discussions, and two other settings she recorded.

The cumulative percentage curves in Figure 2.6 also reveal that in the 12 psychotherapy interviews between JDM and CD, 80 percent of JDM's 793 reaction time latencies were two seconds or less in duration before he spoke. In addition, since such an unusually high latency could not be shown as easily in Figure 2.5, his longest individual reaction time to CD's last utterance over the 12 sessions was 69 seconds. Patient CD's reaction times to him were longer on the average (mean of 4.3 seconds versus his 2.1 seconds), with only 49 percent of hers lasting as little as two seconds or less. Nevertheless, some 75 percent of all her 808 individual reaction time latencies were five seconds or less. Her longest single latency occurred in session seven and was 34 seconds in length. Writers on psychotherapy have long suggested that reaction times before speaking in psychotherapy, either by the patient (client) or therapist, are considerably longer than these upper limits of 34 seconds (CD) and 69 seconds (JDM). In a fuller report on JDM and CD and six additional cases, we have challenged such long-held notions and have encouraged investiga-

2. A start effect in our own duration of utterance distributions shown in the present Figure 2.1 is not revealed because the distribution is plotted in six-second intervals. It is revealed, however, when the data for intervals under six seconds are examined.

tors to substitute data collection for conjecture in describing psychotherapeutic practices (Matarazzo, Wiens, Matarazzo, and Saslow, 1968, pp. 370–371). In the dialogues utilizing normals studied by Jaffe and Feldstein (1970, p. 76) the longest reaction time latency (called "switching pause" by these authors) was only 3.6 seconds. Additionally, in an interesting study designed to extend the range of variables investigated in our studies, Jackson and Pepinsky (1972) report, among other findings, that although their instructed interviewers could successfully answer their clients in less than one second when so programmed, they were unable, in a second part of the same experiment, to wait the required full 10 seconds (responding to the client after only about eight seconds instead).

REACTION TIME LATENCIES IN TWO DIFFERENT SETTINGS

The data from the two-person interviews with each of the 14 supervisor nurses also provides us with an opportunity to contrast the reaction time latency behavior of the nurse in this setting with her reaction time latency behavior in the larger group meeting.

Although plotted only as cumulative percentages, the nursing supervisors' data shown in Figure 2.7 (not previously published) also makes clear that, despite the presence of an L shape in the distribution in each of the two situations, the shorter (faster) reaction times in the group situation clearly reveal that "setting" and "role expectancy" also affect reaction time latency, just as they did the previously described duration of utterance variable. Thus, in the two-person interviews the individual nurse-interviewees responded with a mean reaction time of 2.4 seconds (and median of 0.9 seconds). In contrast, when conversing in a large group of essentially equals, their response was considerably *faster* (mean of only half a second and median of two-tenths of a second). It should be apparent to the reader that study of reaction time latencies (as well as other speech variables) can provide a powerful tool for studying a variety of important human relationships (for example husband-wife, parent-child, roommate-roommate, fraternity faction-fraternity faction, faculty-student, disarmament discussant, congressional committee participant and similar relationships.

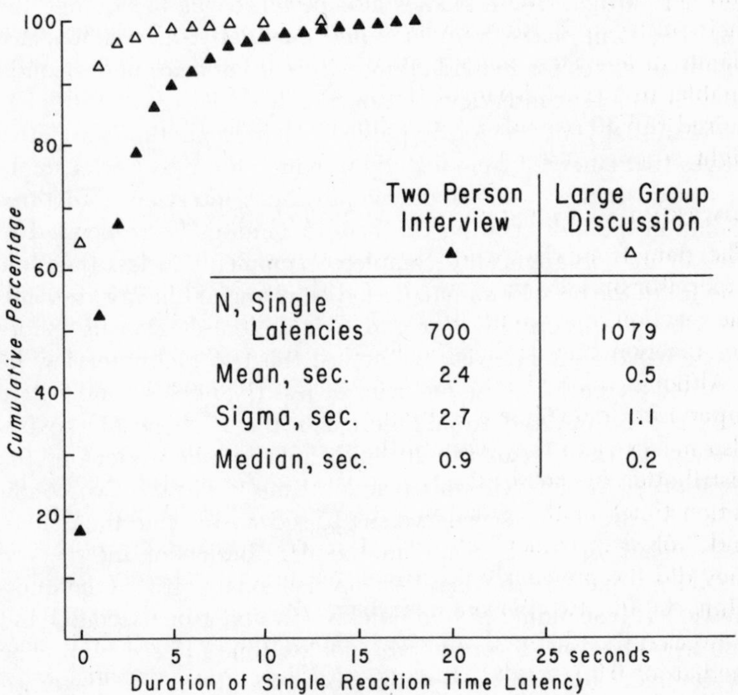

FIGURE 2.7. *Cumulative percentage distribution of single reaction time latencies of supervising nurses in a two-person interview and in discussion among themselves in a large group.*

REACTION TIME LATENCY: INFLUENCE OF DIFFERENT INTERVIEWER REACTION TIME LATENCIES

In a later section we will describe a series of studies in which we quite directly investigated the effect of planned or "programmed" increases and decreases in the interviewer's own reaction time latency upon the reaction time latency of his interviewee-conversational partner. These studies also permitted us to examine the resulting form of the frequency and cumulative percentage distribution curves for individual interviewee latencies under conditions of different interviewer latencies.

Figure 2.8 (not previously published) presents the cumulative curves that emerged from a study in which the interviewer unobtrusively divided a 45-minute employment interview into three 15-minute periods. During the first 15 minutes he responded to each of the job applicant's completed comments in less than one second. In the next 15-minute period he changed this fast responding latency speech behavior and waited 15 full seconds before answering the interviewee. In the last third of each interview he returned to reaction time latencies of less than one second.

As can be inferred from Figure 2.8, the L shape of the frequency distribution of the 20 applicants is independent of the duration of the interviewer's reaction time under the two conditions (his use of one-second versus 15-second reaction time latencies). That is, the L shape in the distribution of *interviewee* latencies appears both when his conversational partner (the interviewer) is responding to him quickly (in under one second) and also when he waits a considerably longer time (15 seconds). The "start effect" also is present under both conditions. The longer reaction time latencies occurring in the presence of the interviewer's own 15-second latencies in Figure 2.8 will be discussed in a later section (Figure 4.9).

Frequency Distributions of Durations of Single Initiative Time Latencies

Another silence duration phenomenon can be observed in two-person conversations and occurs when the second person does *not*

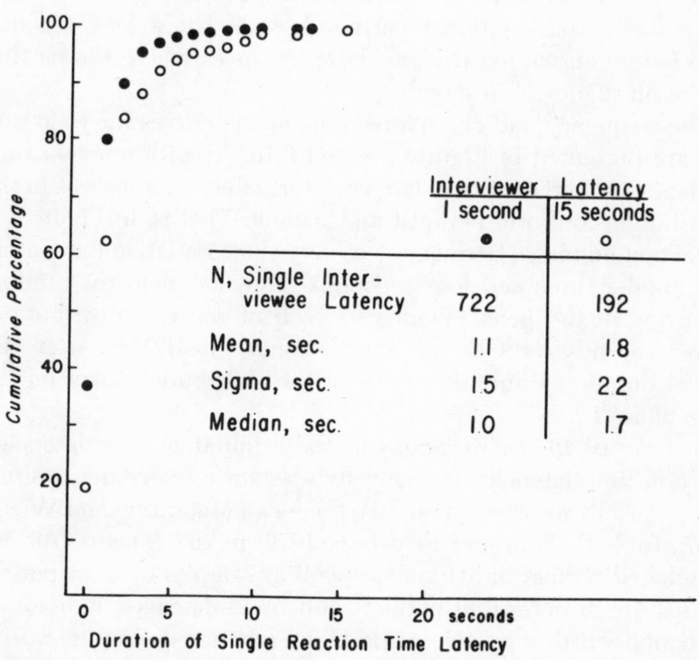

FIGURE 2.8. *Cumulative percentage distribution of single reaction time latencies of different job applicants with one interviewer who modified his reaction time latency durations from one to 15 to one seconds.*

respond in his turn to the first person's completed utterance before the first person speaks again. The duration of time elapsing from a person's just-completed utterance to the moment he initiates with another follow-up utterance of his own is called *initiative time latency.* It occurs much less frequently than does reaction time latency (for example, contrast the numbers of both types represented in Figures 2.5 and 2.9), although its frequency is impressive nevertheless. It occurs more often in those instances where one's conversational partner himself has a long reaction time before answering than in those instances where the partner is himself a "quick" responder.

The frequency and cumulative percentage curves for JDM and CD are presented in Figures 2.9 and 2.10. As with reaction time latencies, an initiative time latency "start effect" is apparent in the distributions of both therapist and patient. That is, in Figure 2.9, the actual number (frequency) of very short initiative time latencies (under three and four seconds) is smaller than the number occurring at the peak (mode) of each of the two distributions (three seconds for CD and four seconds for JDM). After this modal duration value, the shape of the distribution takes on the form of an "L."

In contrast to the durations of these initiative time latencies, reaction time latencies in many two-person conversational situations typically average one to two seconds (Matarazzo and Wiens, 1967, Table 3; Jaffe and Feldstein, 1970, p. 76). This is true for samples of normal individuals as well as samples of most patient groups (with depressed patients and brain-damaged individuals probably constituting two important exceptions). Figure 2.5 reveals that patient CD also is an exception to this typical finding since her mean reaction time latency over the 12 sessions was an unusually high 4.3 seconds. The *means* for the remaining six patients studied along with CD were more typical, however, ranging between 1.72 and 2.21 seconds for the mean of their numerous individual session means (Matarazzo, Wiens, Matarazzo, and Saslow, 1968).

Patient CD's exceptionally long mean reaction time latency notwithstanding, it is probably universally true that each individual's initiative time latency (that is, his reaction time to himself, to

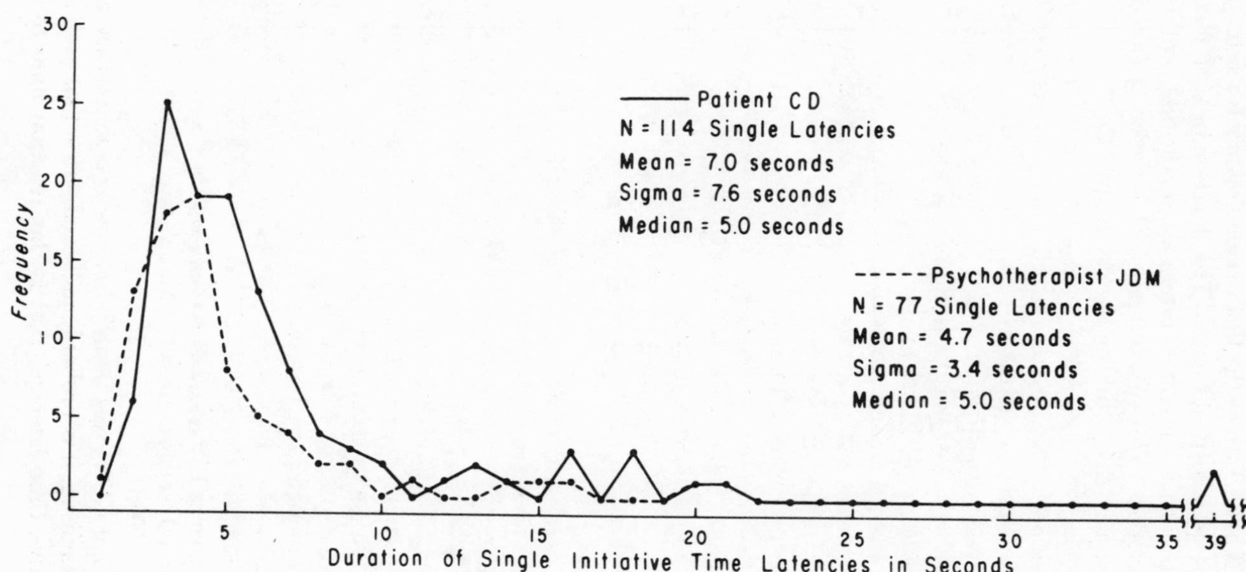

FIGURE 2.9. *Frequency distribution of single initiative time latencies of a psychotherapy patient and a psychotherapist.*

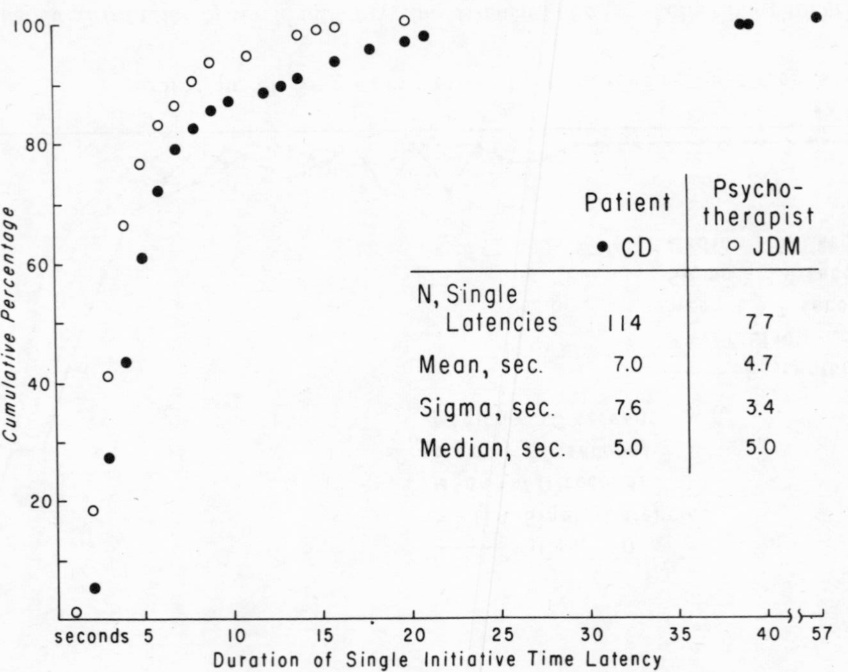

FIGURE 2.10. *Cumulative percentage distribution of single initiative time latencies of a psychotherapy patient and a psychotherapist.*

his own last utterance) is *longer* than is his reaction time latency to a conversational partner. We have, in fact, published extensive data on this point in Matarazzo, Wiens, and Saslow (1965, p. 187) and Matarazzo, Wiens, Matarazzo, and Saslow (1968, p. 356), pointing out in this last study that "Thus, how long the interviewer is willing to wait, five seconds or 15 seconds, profoundly affects the percentage of interviewee initiative, namely, an increase from 25 percent to 65 percent of the time." Lauver, Kelley, and Froehle (1971) report a similar finding of increased initiative responses as reaction time latency increases. This longer initiative time latency relative to reaction time latency can be seen for JDM and CD in the contrast between Figures 2.5 and 2.9. Patient CD had a mean reaction time latency of 4.3 seconds and an initiative time latency in the same 12 sessions of 7.0 seconds. Similarly JDM's comparable interutterance pause durations were 2.1 and 4.7 seconds, respectively.

There may, of course, be exceptions to this generalization that reaction times to one's own last comments typically will be longer than comparable reaction time latencies to the utterances of one's conversational partners. For example, research may reveal that stress associated with arguments or other emotion-laden conversations may be correlated with shorter rather than longer initiative time latencies. This might obtain in those instances where sheer frustration is driving a speaker to pound home his point with numerous quickly formulated initiative comments before his conversational adversary gets a chance to counter with remarks of his own. This last possibility notwithstanding, contrasting the JDM and CD cumulative percentage curves for reaction time latency (Figure 2.6) and initiative time latency (Figure 2.10) underscores the more typical finding.

Frequency Distribution of Interruptions

Our earlier studies have focused on still a fourth variable, *interruptions,* which is a measure of the number of times one speaker begins to speak while his conversational partner is already speaking. It can be expressed as a *frequency,* reflecting the actual number of times an individual begins to speak while another person is already speaking, or it can be expressed as a percentage of the total number of utterances for each speaker.

The interested reader will find a more complete description of the interruption variable in the paper by Wiens, Saslow, and Matarazzo (1966). In that report we presented, among other findings, a frequency distribution curve reflecting the frequency with which 99 heterogeneous inpatient and outpatient psychiatric patients interrupted a psychiatrist-interviewer in a planned five-period interview. These two-person nondirective interviews lasted an average of 32 minutes and followed a format similar to the one employed in the two-person interviews with the supervisory nurses. When plotted as a distribution of raw frequencies, the data of the interrupting speech behavior of the 99 patients formed a mirror-imaged J shape comparable to the one shown in Figure 2.11 (not previously published) and which was obtained from data collected on 18 *staff* nurses who participated in a comparable five-period standardized interview. These nurses, along with fifteen head nurses, served as subjects in the same study as the 14 nursing supervisors (Wiens, Matarazzo, Saslow, Thompson, and Matarazzo, 1965). The eighteen staff nurse two-person interviews lasted an average of 31.9 minutes. During this time the staff nurses made an average of some 66 comments to the interviewer; at the low end of the continuum, one nurse talked 49 times and at the upper end another nurse talked 90 times. They interrupted the interviewer with an average of 6.6 of their mean of 66 utterances, indicating that 10 percent of their comments (actually 9.1 percent due to our dealing with an average of averages) were begun while the interviewer already was speaking. Two of the nurses did not interrupt the interviewer at all, while the staff nurse who interrupted most often interrupted her interviewer-colleague 21 times. Figure 2.11 shows that in their individual interviews eight of the nurses interrupted the interviewer between 0 and 5 times; six between 6 and 10 times; two between 11 and 15 times; one nurse between 16 and 20 times; and one between 21 and 25 times. The resulting distribution of these frequencies is an L shape.

With the exception of thereby revealing the presence or the masking of the "start effect" discussed earlier, the size of the unit

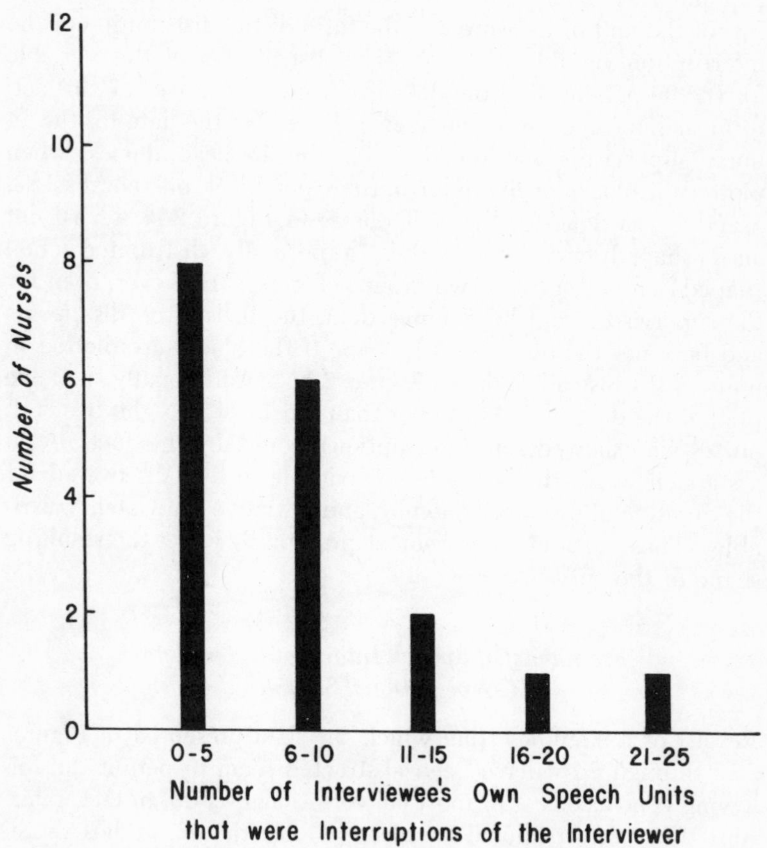

FIGURE 2.11. *Frequency distribution of the number of interruption speech units of a group of staff nurses in a two-person interview.*

chosen for the abscissa (X axis) has, within very broad limits, little bearing on the resulting L shape of the frequency distribution typically obtained for duration of utterance (Figures 2.1 and 2.3) and for duration of the two latency measures (Figures 2.5, 2.7, and 2.9). Such is not the case with the relationship of the size of the unit of measure and the form of the distribution of the interruption variable, however. The distribution of this variable for the 99 patients and the data from the staff nurses do, in fact, form such an L, or mirror-imaged J shape. Yet the data for the 14 nurse supervisors and the data for the 15 head nurses, when plotted in blocks of five interruptions per block on the abscissa, exactly as is done for the staff nurses in Figure 2.11, reveal not an L-shaped curve but, rather, a normally distributed (bell shaped) curve for these two groups of nurses. However, even for the supervisors' and head nurse data, the bell shape disappears and becomes the ubiquitous L shape if the blocks are plotted in units of 10 instead of five (Figure 2.11). Additionally, had we plotted the data in units smaller than blocks of five, the two staff nurses who showed zero interruptions would, by this fact, reveal a start effect for this variable comparable to that discovered for the duration of utterance, latency, and initiative time latency variables. Thus, units of measurement profoundly affect the resulting shape of the curve.

Frequency of Speech Interruptions in Total Conversational Samples

Results of the studies from which the data presented in Figures 2.12 through 2.15[3] have been abstracted seem to permit the following conclusions: (1) most conversationalists do, in fact, interrupt their conversational partner; (2) for the 10 studies repre-

3. For a more complete understanding of Figures 2.12 through 2.15, the interested reader can find full descriptions of the different populations studied and the conditions under which they were studied in the actual reports of each study which are listed in this text and bibliography, or in earlier reviews of the results of these various studies (Matarazzo, Wiens, and Saslow, 1965; Matarazzo, Wiens, Matarazzo, & Saslow, 1968). Accordingly, these descriptions will not be repeated here.

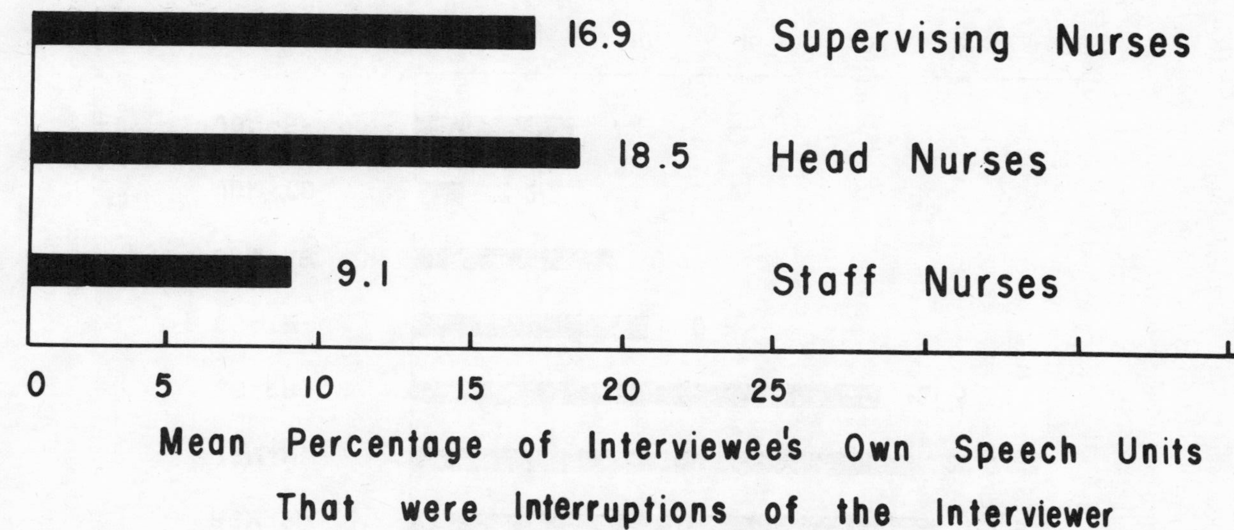

FIGURE 2.12. *Percentage of interruption speech units of three groups of interviewees in a first standardized interview.*

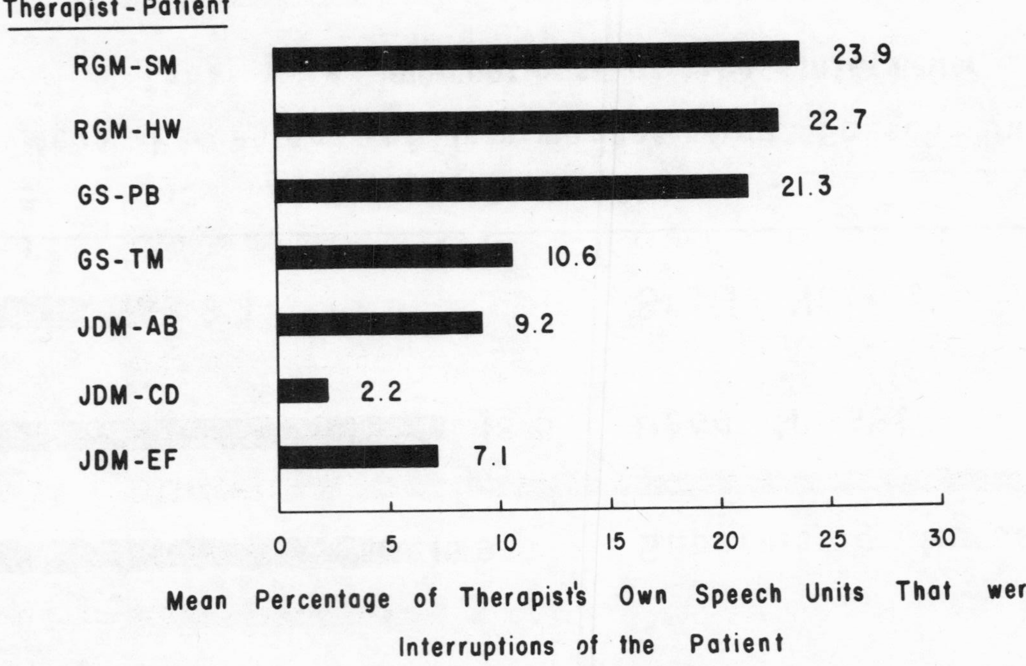

FIGURE 2.13. *Percentage of interruption speech units of three psychotherapists with seven psychotherapy patients over an entire psychotherapy.*

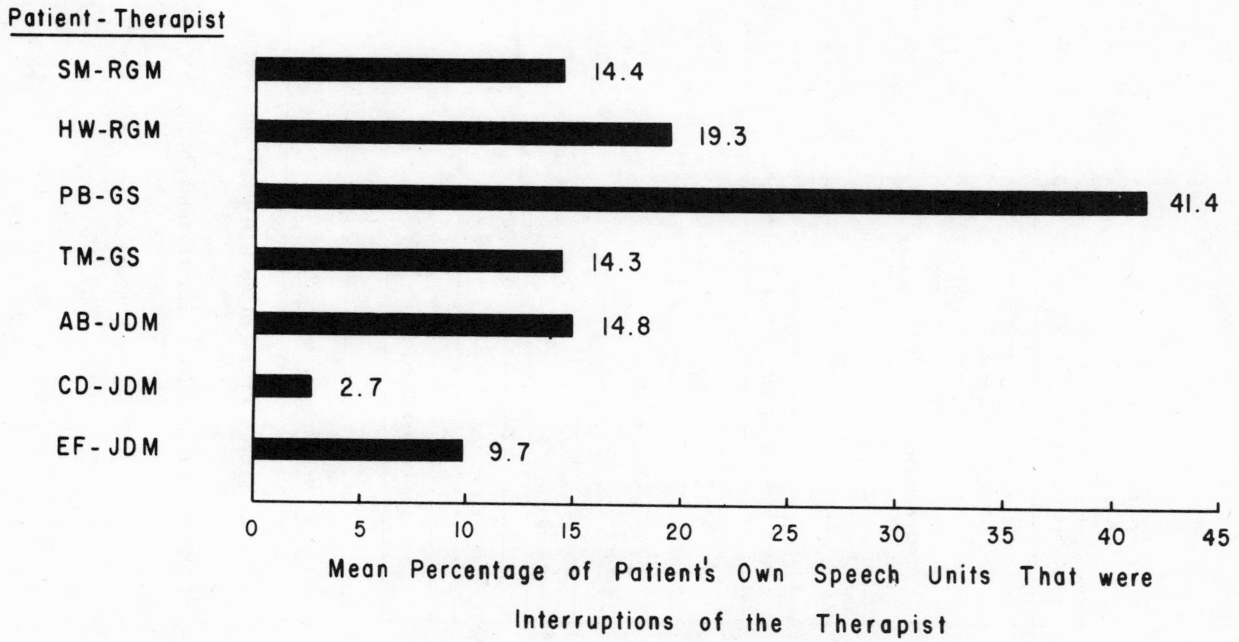

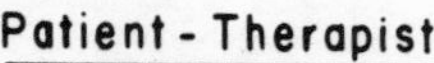

FIGURE 2.14. *Percentage of interruption speech units of seven psychotherapy patients with three psychotherapists over an entire psychotherapy.*

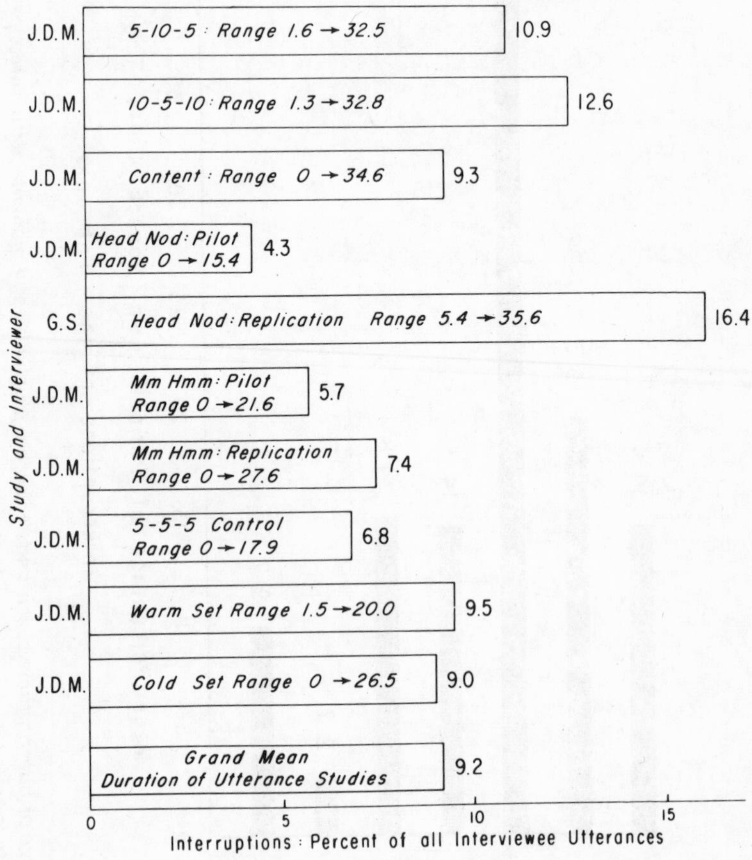

FIGURE 2.15. *Percent interviewee interruptions during interviews.*

sented in Figure 2.15, each consisting of 20 interviewees being interviewed by one interviewer, the range in interrupting behavior among the 20 interviewees represented in *each* study was considerable (that is, wide individual differences in interrupting behavior were found among the interviewees in each study); (3) this *intra*-study variability notwithstanding, there also was considerable study-to-study variability (in Figure 2.15 the mean percent of an interviewee's total number of interruptions ranged from 4.3 in the first (or pilot) Head Nod study to 16.4 in the replication of this same study by a second interviewer); (4) the same interviewer is interrupted differentially by different groups of interviewees (see Figure 2.14, and the JDM studies in Figure 2.15); (5) the same interviewer differs in how often he interrupts different individuals (see Figure 2.13); and (6) administrative status (nurse supervisors and head nurses versus staff nurses) appears to be correlated with how often one interrupts a colleague-interviewer, with staff nurses (lowest on the nursing administrative hierarchy) interrupting the psychiatrist or psychologist-interviewer statistically significantly less often than the two other groups of nurses (9.1 percent versus 16.9 and 18.5 percent, as shown in Figure 2.12).

Whereas some individuals interrupt their conversational partner with almost every other comment they themselves utter (41.4 out of every 100 comments Patient PB in Figure 2.14 uttered interrupted his therapist), most individuals, in the employment interviews represented in Figure 2.15 at least, interrupt considerably less often; averaging a grand mean (mean of the 10 different study means) of 9.2 percent of their own utterances. (Brady [1968] reports that in 16 telephone conversations an interruption occurred in 4.49 percent of the utterances; and Jaffe and Feldstein [1970, p. 128] report a similar 3.2 percent occurrence of interruptions in their dialogues.)

At this point one might ask whether such interruption behavior can be modified by any of a variety of naturally occurring or experimentally induced changes in one or both conversationalists (for example, by changes in his role, setting, mood)? In Chapter 5 (Figures 5.1 and 5.2) we report some conditions that *correlate with* or *modify* how often one speaker interrupts his conversational partner. However, before we examine how speech behavior can be influenced by one's conversational partner it is important that we examine the *stability* of the speech characteristics we have been describing for any individual speaker. How *representative* is one sample of an individual's speech behavior of this same individual's speech behavior in other speaking encounters? Is his average duration of utterance, reaction time latency, and initiative time latency, as well as number (or percentage) of interrupting speech units relatively stable for each speaker? The answer appears to be *yes* if conditions are relatively similar, and *no* if conditions are experimentally changed or the person himself has undergone some important change (for example, role expectancy).

3

Stability in Human Speech Behavior

Stability Studies

Before 1955 very little had been published on the stability (or what some behavioral scientists call the test-retest *reliability*) of interviewee speech behavior; that is, the consistency of interviewee speech or silence characteristics from one interview to a second interview with the same interviewer or other conversational partner. Both Chapple (1949, pp. 300–301) and Goldman-Eisler (1951, pp. 360–362; 1952, p. 671; 1954, p. 178) make passing reference to this problem, and the first extensive study of it was reported by us in a series of five studies published between 1955 and 1959 (Saslow and Matarazzo, 1959). Since 1955 other investigators also have published data on the stability of speech behavior, and their results agree with ours (Mahl, 1956a; Kasl and Mahl, 1956; Cervin, 1956; Tuason, Guze, McClure, and Beguelin, 1961; Kanfer and Marston, 1962; Dinoff, Morris, and Hannon, 1963; Ramsay and Law, 1966; Jaffe and Feldstein, 1970; Conger, 1971; and Jackson and Pepinsky, 1972). Each of these studies attests to the stability of interviewee speech and silence (reaction time latency) durations, especially under controlled conditions of interviewer speaking behavior. Only we and Jaffe and Feldstein (who report r values for the interruption variable) appear to have focused interest on the reliability or representativeness for any given individual of a single sample of his initiative latencies or his interruptions.

Because we also did not recognize the importance of the interruption variable, per se, in these earlier days, we only recently went back and reanalyzed the data of the 99 psychiatric patients comprising these five studies in order to examine its test-retest reliability for any given individual (Wiens, Saslow, and Matarazzo, 1966, Table 2, p. 155).

In addition, the Chapple Interaction Chronograph we used in these five early studies did not permit us to record individual reaction time latencies directly. To abstract these from their parent counters (what Chapple called "tempo" and "activity") required such tedious analysis that we abstracted instead a form of silence duration measure, labeled "silence" by Chapple, which was a composite of each interviewee's reaction time as well as the duration of time the interviewer was speaking (and, of course, the interviewee was still silent in most instances). In view of the fact that the interviewer conducting each of these 99 interviews was programmed (instructed) to conduct his nondirective interview utilizing utterances that were each approximately five seconds in length, this second, or superfluous interviewer-talk-time aspect of the Chapple "silence" variable was a constant value and probably influenced our study of the test-retest reliability of interviewee silence behavior (reaction time latency) minimally, if at all. In a later study of 20 interviews, we specifically investigated this point and found a very high correlation—*r* of .83—between our reaction time latency and Chapple's silence measure (Matarazzo, Hess, and Saslow, 1962, p. 422). Nevertheless it is the Chapple silence variable not reaction time latency, per se, that is presented in Table 3.1 below. Similarly, Chapple's standard scoring approach did not include what we here and elsewhere have been labeling durations of initiative time latency. The Chapple Interaction Chronograph allowed a scorer to abstract the *number* and, thereby, the *percentage* of an interviewee's utterances that were initiative responses. Analysis of durations of such initiative utterances was not part of our methodology in these five early studies. Thus, to remedy this earlier omission, Table 3.1 contains the test-retest reliability for percentage initiative time latency, namely, the percent-

TABLE 3.1. *Test-retest correlations for each of four speech variables in studies utilizing longer and longer intervals of time between the test and retest interview*

		Test-Retest Correlations			
Test-Retest Interval	*Number of Patients*	*Duration of Utterance*	*Silence*	*Percentage Initiatives*	*Number of Interruptions*
Five minutes: 1	20	.91	.76	.81	.73
Five minutes: 2	20	.90	.77	.55	.88
One week	20	.60	.53	.33	.82
Five weeks	19	.86	.78	.83	.73
Eight months	20	.48	.60	.59	.56
Five studies combined	99	.77	.76	.68	.77

age of each interviewee's total number of utterances during a planned *interviewer* wait of 15 seconds that were interviewee initiatives following the interviewee's own last remark.

The results reproduced in Table 3.1 allowed us to draw the following conclusions from the studies we published between 1955 and 1959. (1) There was a striking stability in the speech behavior of each interviewee for each of the four speech variables studied, and this stability obtained whether the two independent interviews were conducted five minutes apart, seven days apart, or five weeks apart; (2) when the interval between the two interviews was increased to eight months, there still obtained a striking, albeit slightly lower index of interviewee similarity (stability) from interview to interview. Interestingly, even in this eight-month interval study, further analyses (Saslow and Matarazzo, 1959, pp. 148–154) indicated that the correlations shown in Table 3.1 for this last study are misleading and that these values mask the fact that 10 of the 20 patients were striking copies of themselves (test-retest correlations of about .95) even after an eight-month interval, whereas the remaining 10 had changed considerably. These further analyses also revealed that the former group of 10 patients (the "nonchangers") had had little psychotherapy in the eight-month interval, while the 10 "changers" had had significantly more hours of psychotherapy.

A word is in order about the conditions under which the 99 pairs of interviews were carried out. In the first and second studies, two interviewers each independently interviewed, five minutes apart, the same new patient (N of 20 interviewees) in an outpatient psychiatric clinic, while an observer, sitting with an Interaction Chronograph behind a one-way mirror, recorded the formal noncontent measures of the interviewer-interviewee interactions. Each interviewer talked about whatever content he typically would in such an initial interview. That is, no attempt was made to standardize the *content* in the two interviews with each patient. However, for reasons that will be clear later (see Figures 4.3 and 4.4), each interviewer was asked to limit each and all of his interview comments to approximately five seconds. The same lack of instructions regarding the content to be discussed in the test and retest interviews, and the five-second interviewer speech duration "rule," obtained in studies 3, 4, and 5, each of which used the *same* interviewer for the two interviews. With such minimal standardization we were able to study the stability of each interviewee's speech characteristics from test to retest interview without concern that the random or idiosyncratic formal speech behavior (of the type of differences shown in Figure 2.13) of the interviewer in the two interviews would introduce a methodological flaw in our research strategy.

Our conclusion from the five studies was that any given interviewee demonstrates strikingly stable speech behavior in the two interviews with a second conversationalist who is talking about different topics in the two interviews but who has "programmed" or "controlled" a few simple dimensions of his own speech behavior. Each of these five studies investigated the test-retest stability of patients as *interviewees*. We and the other investigators cited earlier in this chapter had examined only cursorily the stability in speech behavior of nonpatient interviewees—so-called normals. We felt such a study was necessary for a more thorough understanding of the issue of stability in (or representativeness of) single samples of human conversational characteristics. Consequently, as part of the study of the 14 nursing supervisors shown in Figure 2.3, we decided to retest each of these supervisors a year later so that this question could be examined.

Stability Studies: Nurse Interviewees

Because turnover among nursing supervisors is no less frequent than in other occupational groups, it was not possible for us to decide on an *exact* re-test interval (of 12 months, for example). Rather, with the supervisor who left our medical school for employment elsewhere *only four months after her initial interview,* we reinterviewed her following this relatively brief interval. At the upper extreme, we conducted the second interview with another supervisor after a test-retest interval of 21 months. The mean and median retest intervals for the group were 14.6 and 15.5 months, respectively. In this manner we obtained data on the stability of speech characteristics of 14 normal women, under the same minimally standardized interviewer conditions used with the 99 patients reported in Table 3.1. Information on the age, educational level, and other characteristics of these interviewees may be found in Wiens, Matarazzo, Saslow, Thompson, and Matarazzo (1965).

When we examined the duration of utterance variable for *each* nurse we found, as the reader might infer from the group data shown in Figure 2.3, that the frequency distribution of utterances for each of the nurses was essentially L shaped in each of the two interviews. That is, each nurse tended to have many short utterances and correspondingly fewer utterances of longer and longer duration values. Each individual utterance duration was recorded and a *mean* duration of utterance was obtained for both the first and second interviews for each interviewee. Such a mean (or average) duration of utterance based on all of the individual speech units in a 35-minute interview is a fair index (sample) of this interviewee's utterance durations in this interview. Accordingly, a comparable mean from the second interview permits a fair test of the stability question in this group of normal, nonpatient subjects.

For ease of visual interpretation, the nurse who earned the shortest *mean* duration of utterance in the first interview is plotted first at the top of Figure 3.1 (not previously published). She is followed by the nurse who earned the next highest mean, followed by the nurse with the next highest mean value, until at the bottom of the figure we present the supervisor with the longest mean duration of utterance in Interview 1. These mean values for Interview 1 are shown as a white square for each interviewee. On the *same* line is drawn, as a black square, the mean duration of utterance value in Interview 2. Thus, for example, the supervisor repsented as Interviewee 1 had a mean duration of utterance in her first interview of 18.3 seconds and a mean of 26.1 seconds in her retest interview with the same interviewer. Similarly, Interviewee 11 spoke with a mean duration of utterance of 39.8 and 37.6 seconds, respectively, in her first and second interviews.

Plotting the pairs of means from shortest to longest in Interview 1, as a progression as is done in Figure 3.1, permits the reader to discern *visually* what the unusually high test-retest correlation of .87 (p of .001) also reveals, namely, that even with a test-retest interval of some 15 months the duration of utterance behavior for each of the 14 supervisor-interviewees had remained remarkably stable and unchanged. That is, even though the nurse represented as number 1 clearly is (progressively) different from the nurses at the bottom of the figure, indicating a considerable *range* of individual differences in these interviewees, both she and the other 13 supervisors are each strikingly similar to (or representative of) themselves in their utterance durations in the retest interviews. The data thus demonstrate for this group of nursing supervisors the same degree of stability for duration of utterance (DOU) found for the same variable in the five patient groups shown in Table 3.1.

Examination of the test-retest stability for the remaining three speech variables proceeded along the same lines, and figures ranking the lowest through highest supervisor on each variable were constructed. These are presented as Figures 3.2, 3.3, and 3.4. The results, also not previously published, suggest a fair degree of stability even after an average of 15 months in mean duration of reaction time latency (r of .62, p of .02). However, they reveal only a modest stability in initiative time latency (r of .36, p is not statistically significant), and less stability in the number of times

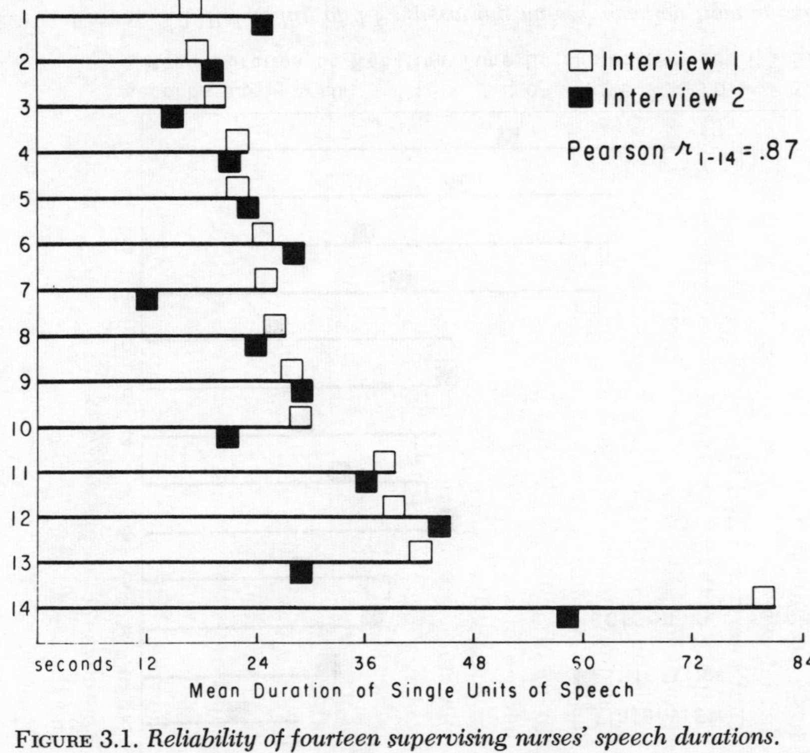

FIGURE 3.1. *Reliability of fourteen supervising nurses' speech durations.*

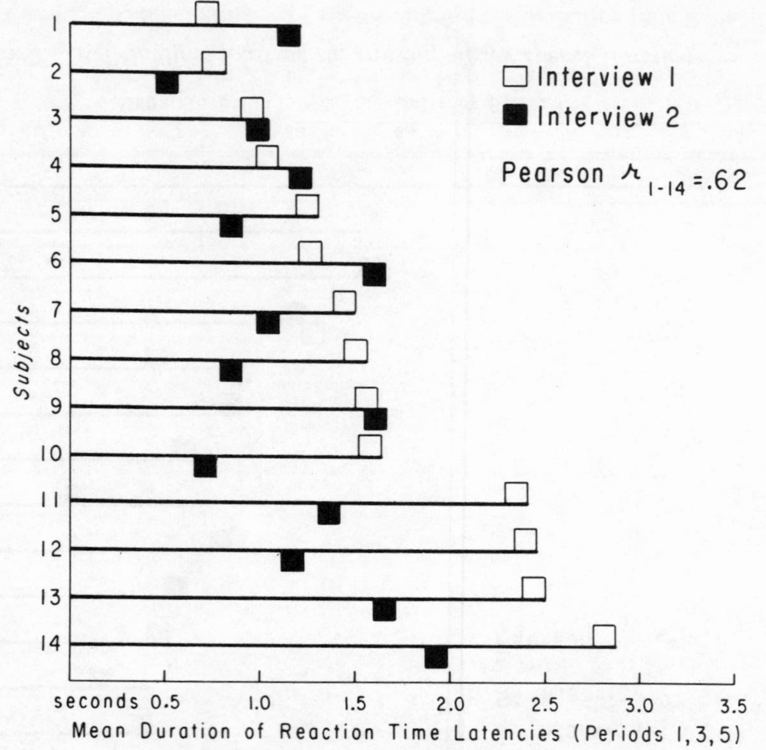

FIGURE 3.2. *Reliability of 14 supervising nurses' reaction time latency.*

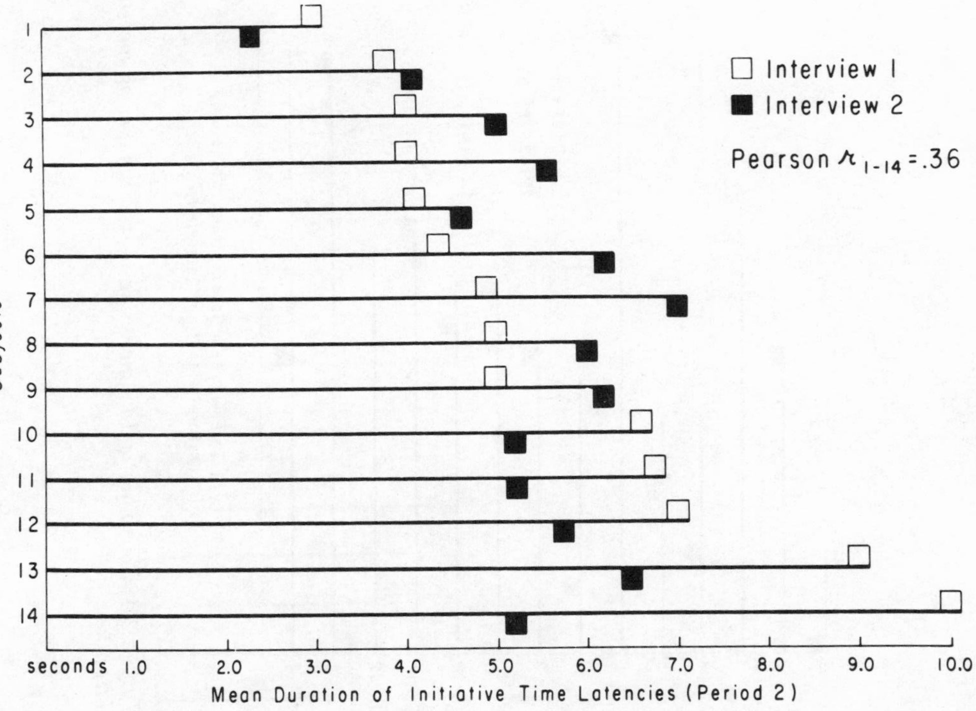

FIGURE 3.3. *Reliability of 14 supervising nurses' initiative time latency.*

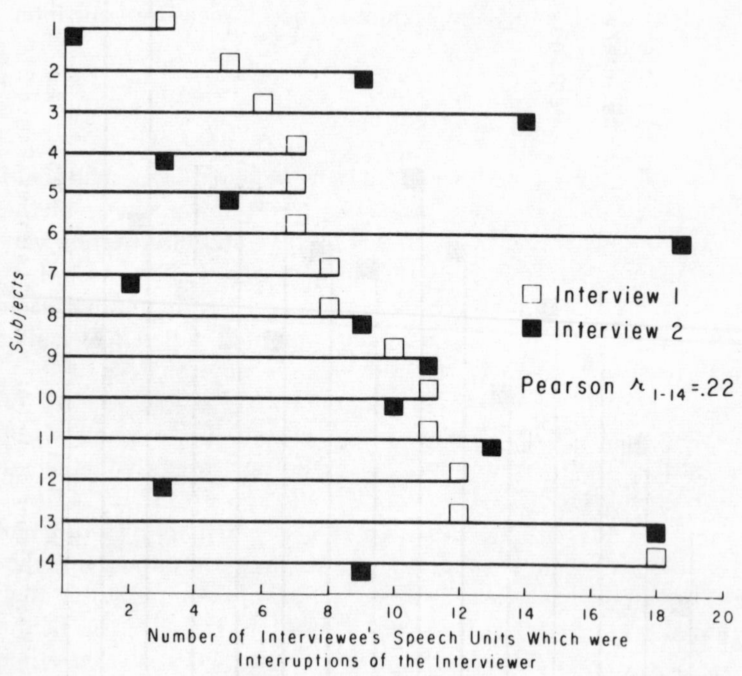

FIGURE 3.4. *Reliability of 14 supervising nurses' number of speech interruptions.*

these supervisors interrupted the interviewer in the two interviews (r of .22, p is not statistically significant). These 15-month test-retest correlations for the two latter variables are considerably lower than those found in the five patient groups shown in Table 3.1. Jaffe and Feldstein (1970) also report in their normal speaker a higher stability for their vocalization and their switching pause measures (in some semblances similar to our DOU and RTL measures) that for their simultaneous speech measure (our interruption measure).

Implications for Further Study

There are many possible explanations or hypotheses that could be proposed to attempt to understand these lower values of the stability index obtained with these initiative and interruption variables and possibly also the reaction time measure. The most obvious of these hypotheses is that, whereas the sum total of each nurse's experiences over a 15-month interval failed to change appreciably her characteristic duration of utterance (r of .87), these same experiences are associated with a modest degree of change in such an interviewee's retest reaction time latencies (r of .62), and much more substantial change in her initiative latencies and interruptions (values of r of .36 and .22, respectively). However, in the various patient groups these two variables did not show so much loss of stability from test to retest after an eight-month interval as shown in Table 3.1. Whereas it is possible that the increase from eight to 15 months before retest is the factor operating in the lower stability values, it occurs to us that other factors also could be operating. One of these is the vulnerability to change, or sensitivity, especially of the initiative and interruption measures, to increased familiarity with the interviewer during the fifteen-month interval obtaining between Interview 1 and Interview 2. Whereas the interviewer conducting all 99 interviews represented in Table 3.1 had no contact with each interviewee (patient) during the test-retest intervals shown, in the nursing study the two interviewers, each of whom interviewed and reinterviewed seven of the nursing supervisors, worked in the same hospital with these interviewees. Thus, while their contact with each supervisor may have been minimal in the test-retest interval, it also may have been enough to modify either the interviewer's "set" or the interviewee's "set" or "expectancies" in the second interview. We unfortunately did not record any such contacts. It is clear, nevertheless, that the findings in Figures 3.1 through 3.4, relative to those in Table 3.1, pose some interesting challenges for further research. For example, in a previous study we and our colleagues reported a *difference* in the speech behavior of two groups of interviewees each of whom had been "given a set" (led to believe) that the interviewer was either a "warm" or "cold" person (Allen, Wiens, Weitman, and Saslow, 1965). Craig (1966); Pope and Siegman (1967); Pierce and Mosher (1967); Kiesler, Mathieu, and Klein (1967); and Truax (1970) also report findings relating to the role of such factors on interviewee speech behavior.

Stability Studies: In the Psychotherapy Setting

Although not collected particularly to answer the question of stability in speech characteristics of normals relative to patients, data from an additional study may help pose questions that might suggest appropriate or potentially promising future research strategies. The numbers of individuals involved is small (three therapists practicing psychotherapy with each of seven patients, with the JDM and CD data shown earlier in Figures 2.1 and 2.2 contributing one of the seven pairs of data). Consequently, in view of the size of the sample, sophisticated statistical analysis of the rank order correlations (rho) obtained with these seven cases was considered superfluous. The data in Table 3.2 are considered suggestive only and represent the stability in the speech variables shown over the seven-day interval between the first and second psychotherapy interview with each patient. The results in this table again suggest considerable stability in the psychotherapists' average utterance and reaction time latency durations and slightly less stability in their percent initiative and number of interruption responses. The two lowest seven-day test-retest correlations for the three nonpatient subjects interacting in *seven* pairs of test-retest interviews were found for the percent interruption (rho of

TABLE 3.2. *Test-retest reliability of patient and therapist speech behavior from first to second interviews*

	Three Experienced Therapists (N = 7)	*Their Seven Patients* (N = 7)
Duration of Utterance	.89	.89
Reaction Time Latency	.90	.60
Initiative Time Latency	–.02	.70
Percent Initiative Utterances	.72	.50
Number of Interruptions	.63	.62
Percent Interruptions	.30	.71
Test-Retest Interval (weeks)	one	

.30) and initiative time latency (rho of –.02) variables. It should be pointed out that, unlike the behavior of the interviewers in the five studies shown in Table 3.1 who were controlling several aspects of their speech behavior, the therapists represented in Table 3.2 were each speaking in their supposedly free, natural psychotherapy manner: their utterances and reaction time latencies could be as short or long as they liked. They also could interrupt, take or not take the initiative, and so on, as they desired. In that sense, then, they were as free to behave naturally as were the 14 nurse-interviewees represented in Figures 3.1 through 3.4. The data for the same four nurse variables reveal correlations for the nurse data (.87, .62, .36, and .22, respectively), which are roughly similar to the comparable therapist correlations for the same variables (.89, .90, –.02, and .63) shown in Table 3.2.

This comparison of findings in two nonpatient samples again reveals that for these "normal" individuals the initiative latency variable is subject to change, whether the interval be 15 months or seven days. However, the therapist correlations, both the strong and the weak ones, reported in Table 3.2 can be at most suggestive, since they were not computed from strictly laboratory research data, but are the *byproducts* of a serious clinical encounter (the clinical psychotherapeutic interaction), which was the chief concern of each therapist.

The stability correlations shown also for the seven patients in Table 3.2 are of interest because their order of magnitude for the various speech variables is roughly similar to comparable correlations shown for the five larger groups of patients represented in Table 3.1.

These results from our several reliability studies led us to conclude that, under comparable interview conditions, a fair degree of test-retest stability exists in most of the speech variables we had been investigating. However, from the first test-retest reliability study we conducted in 1954 to 1955, we were obtaining important evidence that, no matter how much stability we were discovering under conditions that were roughly identical, the various speech variables *were susceptible* to influence. These observations, first reported by Chapple (1949, pp. 300–301) and confirmed by us even in *subperiods* of each of the 99 early reliability interviews (Matarazzo, Saslow, Matarazzo, and Phillips, 1958), led us, as well as Jaffe and Feldstein (1970), Heller (1968, 1971), Pope and Siegman (1970), and others, to begin a program of research directed quite explicitly toward discovering conversational and other variables that could influence the speech behavior of one's partner. The last sections of this volume will focus on these studies of ours. However, before leaving this early section devoted to individual differences among interviewees in speech characteristics, it might be of interest to examine in summary fashion the differences *between* groups of interviewees representing different patient and normal samples. We have published more detailed reports on some of these samples, and the interested reader is referred to them (Matarazzo and Saslow, 1961; Matarazzo, 1962; Matarazzo, Wiens, and Saslow, 1965; Wiens, Matarazzo, Saslow, Thompson, and Matarazzo, 1965; and Molde and Wiens, 1967).

Individual Differences among Groups

It should be clear from the duration of utterance mean values shown for the 14 supervisors that even within this apparently homogeneous occupational sample there is a wide range of differences in the individual mean values from one nurse to the next. Nevertheless, if we compute the average (median) value of the

14 individual mean durations of utterance for the group as a whole, we find that the value (for the first 14 interviews) is 28.5 seconds. These interviews were conducted with the 14 supervisors under a standardized interview schedule consisting of five periods and first introduced by Chapple (Matarazzo, Saslow, and Matarazzo, 1956).

For purposes of the next comparison it is fortunate that we interviewed a variety of normal and patient groups utilizing this *same* five-period standardized interview. Since the interviewer's behavior along the relevant formal speech dimensions (he was instructed to speak in utterances of five seconds each time he spoke) was similar in each interview and from group to group, *intergroup* comparisons are clearly permissible. Where available, we will report median values rather than means for the groups because medians are less susceptible than means to distortion by scores of one or two exceptionally deviant individuals. In that sense the medians are a better index of group data for the type being compared here. Median values were not computed for the interviewer duration of utterance in these early studies, and the raw data no longer are available for analysis. Nevertheless, from inspections of the means and distributions it seems fair for us to conclude that for each group the interviewer was within a fraction of a second of a median of five seconds. Thus for the first five (early) groups in Figure 3.5 we show a value of 5.0 for these medians.[1]

There *are* clear differences in the characteristic (or average) duration of utterance from one group to the next. In earlier publications (Matarazzo and Saslow, 1961; Wiens, Matarazzo, Saslow, Thompson, and Matarazzo, 1965), we have reported finding statistically significant differences between the *means* of (1) each of the three patient groups at the top of Figure 3.5 and each of two groups of normal sales personnel-interviewees (the latter are omitted because we did not interview them), and (2) the staff nurses and each of the two administrative nurse groups (head nurses and supervising nurses) shown at the bottom of the figure. More elaborate or comprehensive analyses of *inter-group* differences

1. The reader will find the actual *means* published in our earlier studies.

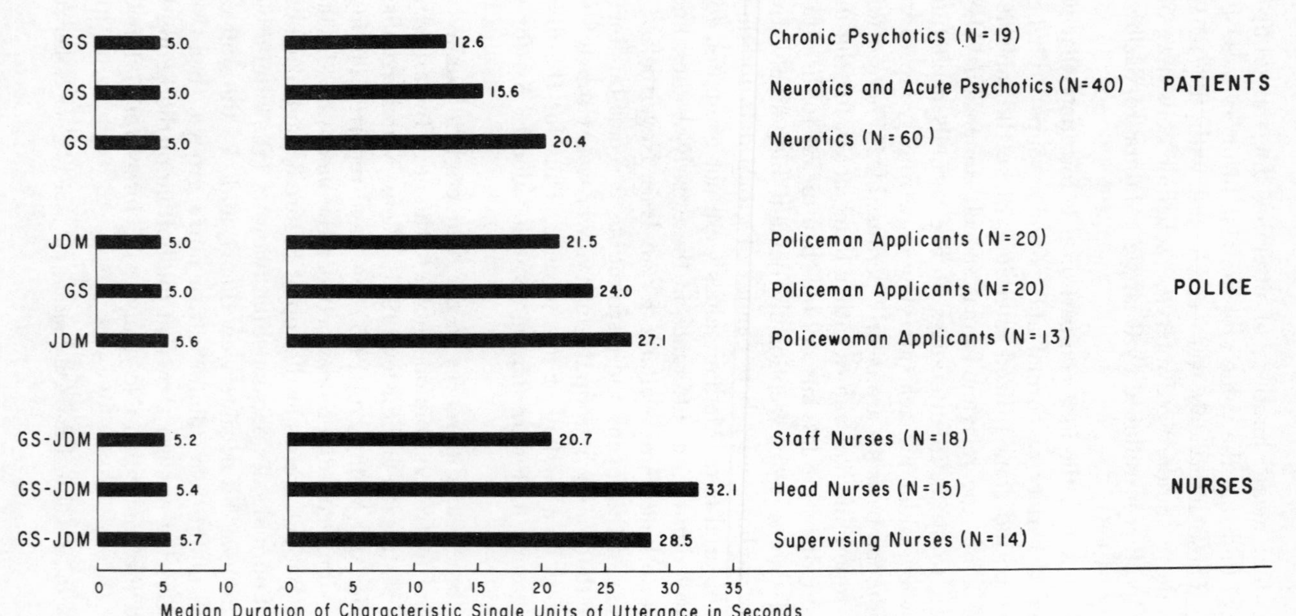

FIGURE 3.5. *Duration of interviewee speech in a five-period standardized interview.*

were not carried out on the data because, while differences in median or mean values are of interest in themselves, the intragroup *variability* within each and every single group shown was so large as to be possibly more important than the intergroup differences themselves. Figure 3.1 shows these *intragroup* individual differences for the 14 supervisory nurses; and an earlier publication (Matarazzo & Saslow, 1961) shows them for the three patient groups at the top of Figure 3.5. This fact of considerable *intra*group variability notwithstanding, it is our belief that the *inter*group differences may offer suggestive leads for further exploration by interested behavioral scientists and others interested in interview behavior. However, we ourselves did not have the resources to follow these leads further. It is our conviction, nevertheless, that objective indexes such as the utterance duration variable shown offer a more promising approach to diagnostic classification and the corollary understanding of important personality differences among individuals than has been offered by the traditional psychiatric-psychologic approaches used heretofore. A more complete explication of this point has been presented elsewhere (Matarazzo, 1965, pp. 440–445).

Nathan, Schneller, & Lindsley (1964) have also reported analogous data from interviews with patients newly admitted to a state hospital. Those patients less severely ill had higher rates of talking with their interviewer, and patients talked less when discussing personally related and stressful content. Kanfer (1960) found, for example, that female psychiatric patients spoke at a rate (90 words per minute) that was 25 percent slower when talking with an interviewer about how they reacted to members of the opposite sex than when they talked about their present illness (120 words per minute). Craig (1966) similarly reported differences in the DOU and RTL speech behavior of psychiatric patients when the interviewer was giving them interpretations of their personality state that were congruent with their own perceptions, versus interpretations that were incongruent. Kanfer (1960) and Pope, Blass, Siegman, and Raher (1970) studying psychosomatic patients (none were psychotic) and recording periodic free-speech monologues, found differences in speech and silence behavior in clinically rated states of increased anxiety versus rated states of depression. In another study, based on interview data from normal subjects, Pope, Siegman, and Blass (1970) demonstrated related differences in speech behavior under anxiety-stimulated versus neutral conditions. The implications for further studies are legion.

The data in Figure 3.6, may suggest further *intergroup* comparisons, and are shown in means (as published). The interviewee samples, grouped by differences in sex (policemen and policewomen) and administrative hierarchy (staff versus head and supervisory nurses), were each interviewed using Chapple's five-period standardized interview. Conversely, the two nurse samples grouped by specialty (surgical versus psychiatric) were interviewed by Donald Molde (DM) using a 30-minute interview with only one period. That is, DM continued Chapple's Period 1 for a full 30 minutes, thereby leaving out Chapple's next four periods (Molde and Wiens, 1967). Nevertheless, the surgical nurse and psychiatric nurse specialty groups each were interviewed by a single interviewer (DM) using the *same* interview conditions with each. The group meeting data shown at the bottom of Figure 3.6 come from unpublished studies in which we recorded the speech behavior of two groups of nursing personnel who differed along an administrative-professional hierarchy (practical and registered nurses) and who were meeting *together* in weekly group meetings and two additional groups of nurses who differed only on the administrative hierarchy (head nurses and supervising nurses) and who also met together monthly in a single group. The *intergroup* comparisons are heuristically provocative. It would appear, although we did not carry out such analyses, that the higher the administrative or professional role or status of the nurse, the longer is the average duration of utterance for such a nurse under these group conditions. Numerous additional interpretations and hypotheses for further studies are possible, but we are concentrating our investigative efforts elsewhere for the moment, although we feel confident the data are sufficiently suggestive that their implications should be explored. As a matter of fact, Jaffe and Feldstein (1970, p. 42 and pp. 138–140) report some interesting sex differences in speech behavior that can be added to the suggestive leads at the top of Figure 3.6 and Figure

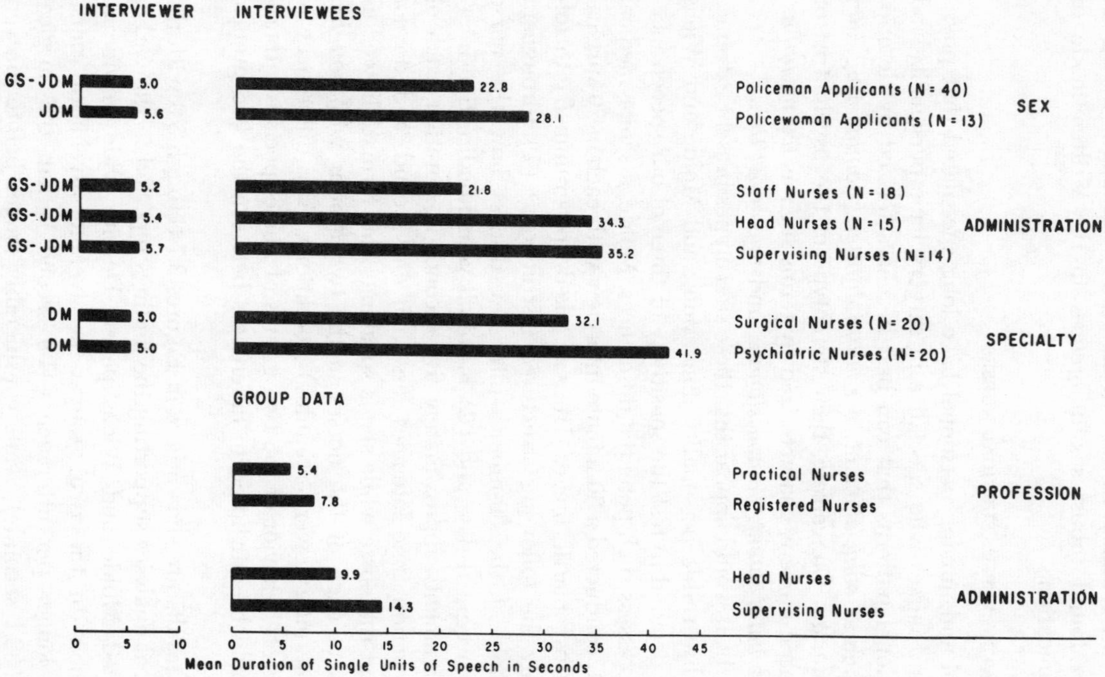

FIGURE 3.6. *Mean duration of utterance for seven groups of interviewees and four groups of discussion participants.*

2.13 (in which one therapist is female and two therapists are male) and Figure 2.14 (in which two patients are male and five patients are female). In our own laboratory Manaugh (1971) has recently found robust sex differences in the written mode of communication.

PSYCHIATRIC VERSUS SURGICAL NURSES

Medical and nursing personnel have long speculated that physicians and nurses who specialize in surgery have personality and professional patterns that can best be characterized by descriptions such as *cold, efficient, verbally inhibited, domineering,* and *authoritarian.* Conversely, their stereotype of the psychiatrist or psychiatric nurse is characterized by terms such as *warm, unhurried, verbally fluent, compassionate,* and *uncompetitive.*

Clearly, it would appear that these stereotypes present extremes along discernible personality dimensions, and Molde and Wiens (1967) decided to test the sensitivity of three of our speech measures to assess such potential differences. Molde, a senior medical student, conducted a 30-minute interview with each of 20 surgical and 20 psychiatric nurses. He was asked (programmed) to follow only the following structured instructions: (1) throughout the whole of the 30-minute interview discuss how the nurse spends a typical day; and (2) make all your nondirective interview comments approximately five seconds in duration, each of your reaction time latencies less than one second, and do *not* interrupt the nurse while she is speaking. This format allowed us to present each of the nurses in the two groups with *roughly identical* interviewer (stimulus) conditions. Any differences in the speech behavior of the two groups of nurse-specialists therefore could be attributed to differences between the two groups, per se.

The results are shown here in Figures 3.7 through 3.9 with the statistical analyses supporting the findings reported in the earlier published Molde and Wiens paper. Despite wide *intragroup* differences in the two groups, the average psychiatric nurse speaks longer per utterance (41.9 seconds) than the surgical nurse (32.1 seconds), waits considerably longer before answering the interviewer (.96 versus .57 seconds), and interrupts

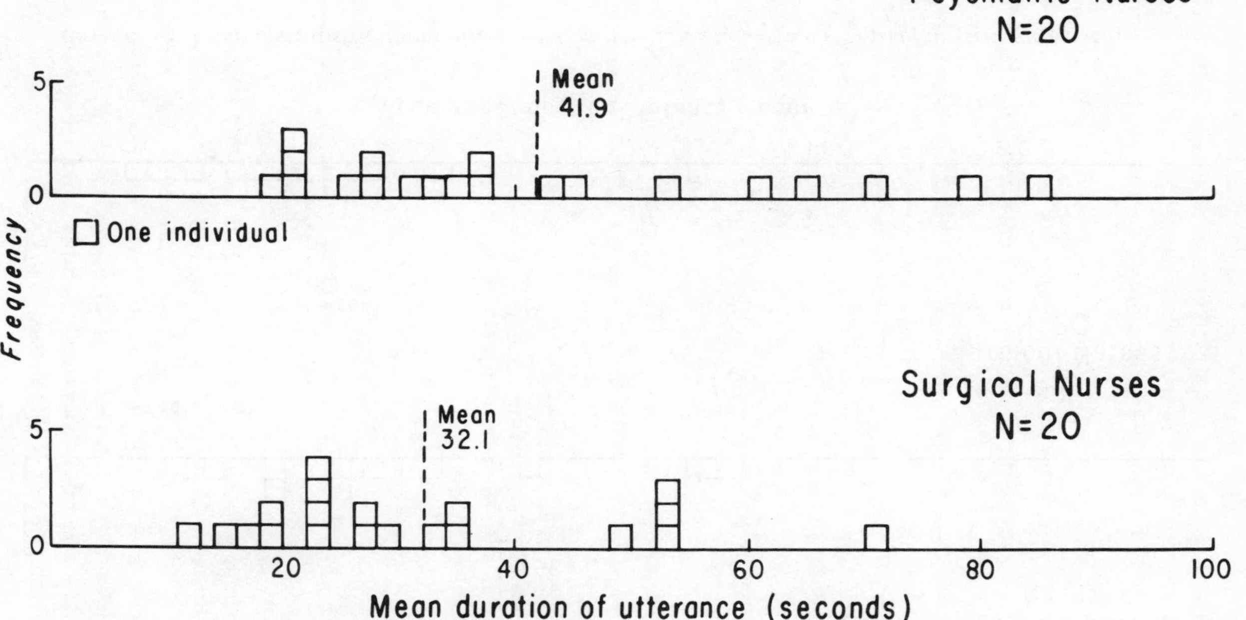

FIGURE 3.7. *Frequency distribution: mean duration of utterance for two groups of nurse interviewees.*

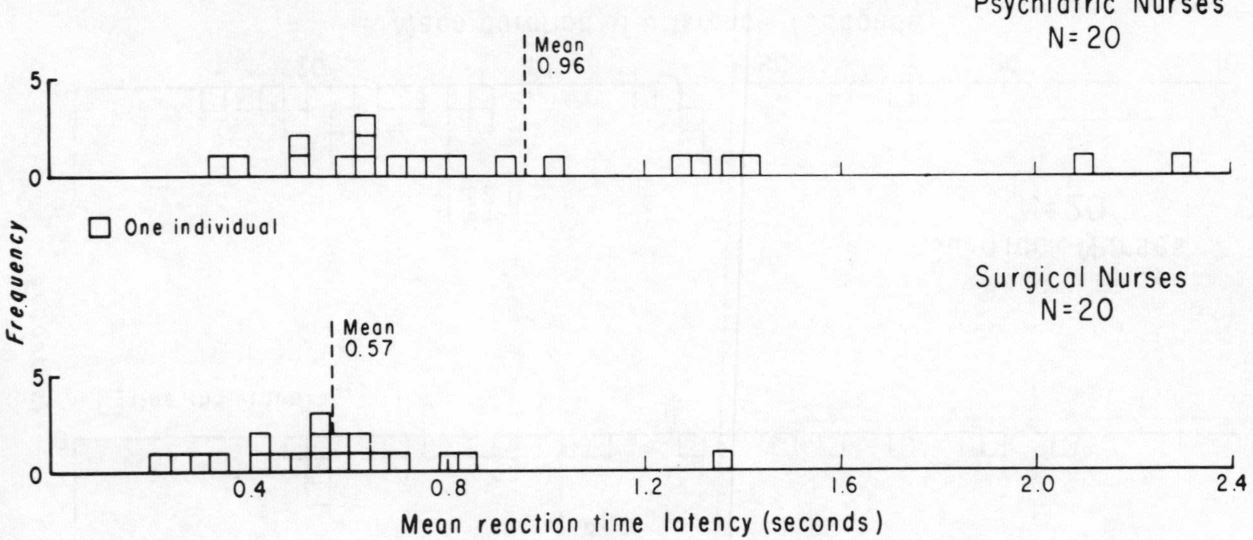

FIGURE 3.8. *Frequency distribution: mean reaction time latency for two groups of nurse interviewees.*

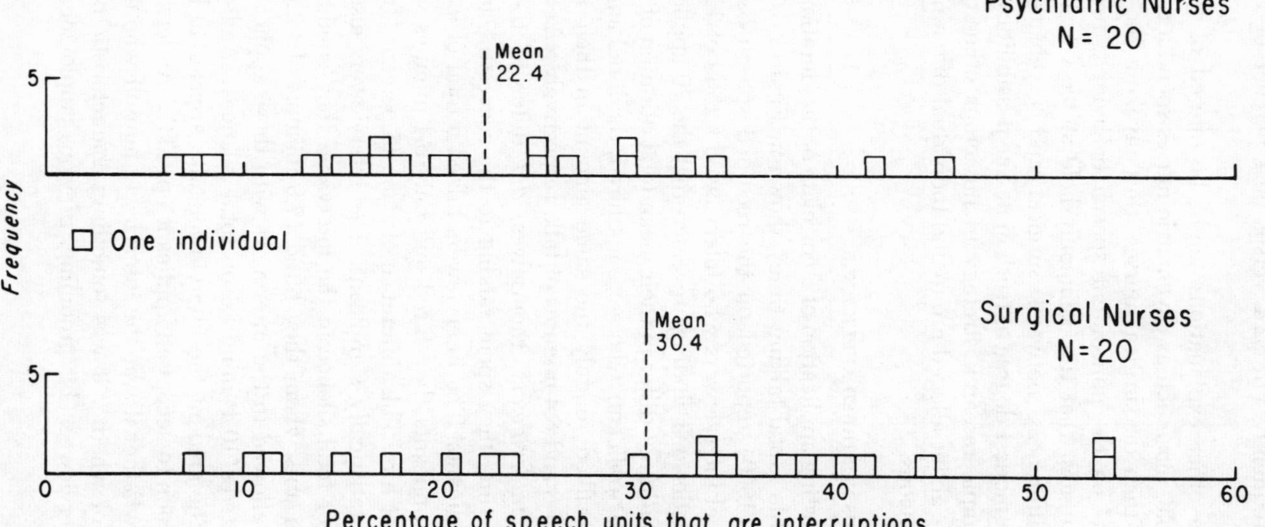

FIGURE 3.9. *Frequency distribution: percentage of speech units that are interruptions for two groups of nurse interviewees.*

him less frequently (in 22.4 versus 30.4 percent of their own utterances).

Although other explanations might be offered of the results (for example, inasmuch as psychiatric nurses spend a typical day differently than do surgical nurses—thus invoking the influence of "content" on the noncontent speech behavior), these results may also suggest that the commonly held stereotype about personality differences between surgical and psychiatric nurses may have a modest degree of truth in it. The possibilities of applying this simple research strategy to numerous other commonly held beliefs about alleged group and individual differences hopefully are obvious.

HIRED VERSUS NONHIRED APPLICANTS

In an interesting application of a correlate of the duration of utterance variable (total talking time) shown in Figures 3.5 and 3.6, Anderson (1960) reported on the recorded speech behavior of six personnel interviewers who interviewed a total of 115 job applicants. Anderson's findings revealed that the 70 applicants who were hired *did not* differ in their mean total duration of utterance from the 45 applicants who were not hired; the hired and rejected applicants talked roughly the same amount in their interviews (means of 7.8 and 8.4 minutes of talk, respectively). Yet, interestingly, the *interviewers,* themselves, *did* differ in the average amount of time they spent talking to the successful and unsuccessful applicants! The interviewers talked a total of 9.3 minutes with the applicants they hired and only 6.4 minutes with those they did not hire. This difference of some 45 percent (from 6.4 to 9.3) was statistically significant. The interviewers also allowed *less* time for total silence in the interviews they conducted with those applicants whom they hired (7.9 minutes of total silence) than they allowed in the interviews with those applicants whom they rejected (10.4 minutes of total silence). Anderson concluded: "The amount the interviewer talks appears to be related to his decision to accept an applicant (p. 268)." Anderson did not speculate whether it was the interviewer himself who decided to talk more or whether it was something characteristic of the successful interviewee (his grooming, previous employment history, and so on) that elicited greater talk from his potential employer. Such questions notwithstanding, if Anderson's findings can be confirmed by other investigators, the implications of such findings for the dating and courtship relationship, employer-employee, roommate-roommate and other peer relationships, as well as parent-child, teacher-child, spouse-spouse, sergeant-private, and other important and common human pair relationships would appear considerable.

4

Modifiability in Human Speech Behavior

We were fortunate that when we started our program of research we used Chapple's five-period standardized interview as our standard for studying the reliability across the *total* approximately 30-minute interview of our (four) speech variables. Had we used, for example, a 30-minute interview that, for both the test and retest sample, required only one "period," throughout which the interviewer's behavior remained *stable and invariant,* we might easily have missed discovering what we feel has been the most interesting and possibly significant finding of our overall research program: namely, that despite the demonstrated test-retest stability of these conversational speech attributes (discovered under conditions of comparable stimulus input), these same speech characteristics (the interviewee's output) can be *dramatically changed* for a given interviewee by the simple procedure of introducing relevant changes in the speech behavior of his conversational partner (for example, the stimulus input from the interviewer).

Chapple's early five-period standardized interview format programmed the interviewer, for example, to respond to the interviewee with one-second reaction time latencies in Periods 1, 3, and 5, but to modify this drastically in Period 2 (wherein he increased his reaction time latencies to 15 seconds each) and also in Period 4 (wherein he decreased his reaction time latencies to "negative" values in the sense that he did *not* wait for the interviewee to complete an utterance but, rather, systematically *interrupted* him even while the interviewee-patient was still talking). Beginning with the first, and continuing in each of the additional test-retest reliability studies, we were able to investigate the effects upon the interviewee's speech behavior of planned and standardized changes such as these in the interviewer's own *intra-interview* speech behavior across the five periods. The results, although a byproduct of the test-retest reliability question we were then actively investigating but, nevertheless, first systematically acknowledged in two early papers (Matarazzo, Saslow, Matarazzo, and Phillips, 1958, and Matarazzo, 1962), were quite striking: as the interviewer experimentally changed his own duration of utterance and duration of reaction time latency from one period of the interview to another, there were striking and reproducible changes in the speech behavior of the patient-interviewees. These incidental findings led us to outline a series of more rigorously controlled studies that were designed to investigate more systematically the types of interviewer (input) variables that could bring about these changes in the speech behavior (output) of the conversational partner (the interviewee).

These studies constitute our main investigative interest since roughly 1959 to 1961. During this same period of time another fortuitous event occurred: we were asked to participate in the selection of job applicants for the position of patrolman in a large city in the Northwest. Our responsibility involves a full day of intensive psychological assessment of each applicant. Active participation in this undertaking over the past 13 years has provided us with a continuing sample of young men whose age, educational, intellectual, personality, and motivational characteristics have been remarkably stable[1] from one year to the next. The vari-

1. The characteristics of the patrolman-applicant interviewees in these 15 to 20 separate studies since 1959 are approximately as follows: mean age (25.7 years), mean education (12.6 years), mean IQ (112, 80th percentile) emotional stability and maturity (high), and motivational level (high). The interested reader can find a more complete description of these applicants in one of our earlier reports (Matarazzo, Allen, Saslow, and Wiens, 1964).

ous individual studies summarized in this section are directly comparable to each other for this reason.

Duration of Utterance: Modifiability Studies

We have carried out some eight separate studies, each involving 20 applicant-interviewees, in order to examine the interviewer (input) variables that it was hypothesized could reliably influence the interviewee's average duration of utterance (output) within designated portions of a single interview. The general character of this standardized 45-minute interview (see one actual interview in the appendix) follows that of a fairly typical clinical-employment interview of the type employed by professional interviewers of executives, military officers, foreign service officers, applicants for admission to medical school, and so on. Such interviews follow a pattern of a rather free-flowing, psychosocially oriented interview and thus have characteristics in common with both the employment and the psychiatric interview. Unknown to the interviewee, the interview was divided into three 15-minute periods. Additionally, and in order not to have interview content (the specific topic areas discussed) vary randomly from interviewee to interviewee and thus operate as a potential contaminating variable, interview content was *standardized* for all interviewees into the same three broad categories: occupation (O), education (E), and family (F) history. During *each* 15-minute period the interviewer, using nondirective open-ended questions, encouraged the applicant to discuss personal history data from these same three content areas, devoting approximately 5 minutes to each of the three content areas in each of the three 15-minute periods. In order to permit the interviewer to remain spontaneous, he was not required to introduce each 5-minute content sequence in the same order each time, although our experience indicated that it was fairly easy for him to stick rather closely to an OEF–OEF–OEF design for content across the 9 5-minute segments for each of the 20 applicants in the various studies described here. Parenthetically, we have conducted separate studies to examine explicitly the influence of specific *content* on interviewee speech behavior (see Appendix), and these will be reported in Chapter 6.

Because the earlier test-retest reliability studies had suggested the incidental finding that changes in the interviewer's own duration of utterance (DOU) could produce analogous changes in the duration of utterance of his interviewees, this (DOU) variable was chosen as one of the first to be investigated more systematically.

THE 5–10–5 STUDY

This was the first study in the new series, and utilized the 45-minute interview described above. The interviewer in this study systematically *varied* his own durations of utterance during the interview in the following manner: (1) for the first 15 minutes each of the interviewer's single units of seemingly normally and spontaneously flowing speech was always of 5 seconds' duration (plus or minus a few tenths of a second); (2) for the second 15 minutes his individual comments were always of 10 seconds' duration; and (3) for the third 15 minutes his speech was once again always of 5 seconds' duration. Use of the OEF–OEF–OEF content procedure further insured that random variations in content across these three 15-minute periods from one interviewee to another *would not* be present to introduce an additional variable in unknown ways, thus helping to insure the operation of only one variable (5-second versus 10-second interviewer utterance durations).

With a few practice interviews an interviewer (either novice or experienced) can learn to conduct smooth flowing, nondirective interviews *exclusively* in, for example, 5-second utterances or 10-second utterances. To do this requires merely a little practice and the added information that two sentences (one general, summarizing, or reflecting and the second open-ended) consume approximately five seconds to verbalize. (For example: "Now, Tom, you have told me a little about your high school record. I wonder if you would describe how your parents felt about these grades?" Numerous additional examples appear in the transcribed interview of one such interview given in the Appendix of this volume.)

In the 5–10–5 and each of the other duration of utterance studies, the interviewer was instructed to remain spontaneous, never to interrupt the applicant, in each instance to respond to the applicant's last comment with a reaction time latency of one second or less, and to maintain a relatively neutral facial and bodily expression throughout the whole interview. These last requirements (programmings) have seemed empirically in no way to constrain the spontaneity of the interviewer. They were introduced for the 5–10–5 and all subsequent studies because we guessed, and our later research confirmed, that any of a number of interviewer-emitted tactics or other cues can be reinforcing (markedly influential in inducing a change in the interviewee's speech behavior). We hoped to systematically study, as much as possible, each of these variables, and one at a time, rather than have them operate "randomly" in each or any of the studies.

The effects on the interviewees of the interviewer's planned changes in his own duration of utterance over a 5–10–5 experimental range will be presented shortly. However, the reader will better understand the results of that study and the others in this subsection if he first becomes acquainted with the speech behavior of a group of 20 job applicants who were interviewed by an interviewer who did *not* modify his behavior from one 15-minute period to the next in such an otherwise similarly standardized 45-minute interview. This group is called a *control group* in our various figures.

CONTROL GROUP (5–5–5): DURATION OF UTTERANCE.

We earlier have reported (Matarazzo, Wiens, and Saslow, 1965, pp. 193–194) that an interviewer who interviewed another group of 20 of these job applicants as a control group by utilizing a *planned* 5–5–5 second duration of utterance schedule did, in fact, empirically obtain mean durations of utterance for himself across the three periods of 5.0, 5.2, and 5.2 seconds, respectively. Such stable and nonchanging speech durations on his part elicited comparably stable and unchanging mean speech durations from his 20 interviewees: 30.0, 30.5, and 28.1 seconds, respectively. Thus, as his speech behavior (input) remained constant across the three 15-minute periods so did that of his conversational partners (output).

We have recently completed interviewing a second (5–5–5-second) control group of 20 applicants and, since the results have not been previously published, they will be presented here to help the reader better understand the speech variable under discussion. The interview schedule and "programmed" instructions followed by the interviewer were identical to those followed in Control Group 1; namely, in *each* of the three periods he was never to interrupt, was to answer the applicant in less than one second, and to do so with a five-second utterance. The results for the interviewer and each of his 20 interviewees are given in Table 4.1. The *mean* durations of utterance shown in this

TABLE 4.1. *Interviewer's and interviewee's mean duration of single utterances across three 15-minute periods of one interview: Control group 2*

	Interviewer's (JDM) Mean Duration of Each Utterance				Interviewee's Mean Duration of Each Utterance			
	periods				periods			
subject	1	2	3	p	1	2	3	p
1	5.0	5.3	5.0		17.6	15.6	13.5	
2	4.7	4.9	5.5		17.9	19.2	20.2	
3	4.7	4.7	5.3		32.9	35.4	33.7	
4	4.9	4.6	5.0		48.2	35.2	62.2	.01
5	5.2	4.6	4.2	.05	44.0	62.9	47.6	
6	4.8	4.8	4.7		39.8	34.4	50.0	
7	4.9	4.1	4.5		50.5	48.6	56.0	
8	4.8	5.0	5.4		61.4	30.9	49.4	.05
9	4.4	5.0	5.2		24.6	26.0	44.9	.05
10	4.7	4.9	4.6		25.7	32.4	18.5	.01
11	5.1	5.3	4.7		33.3	36.8	35.7	
12	5.2	4.7	5.2		69.8	82.9	68.2	
13	4.8	5.2	5.2		45.7	39.2	33.9	
14	5.3	5.6	5.7		54.3	67.3	52.3	
15	5.3	5.4	4.6		65.2	76.9	91.9	
16	4.8	4.7	5.5		38.3	45.5	47.4	
17	4.7	4.9	5.0		29.6	38.7	25.0	
18	4.9	4.6	4.6		26.3	20.5	27.8	
19	5.8	6.0	5.0	.05	30.6	31.1	37.2	
20	5.5	6.3	5.5		56.8	30.8	20.5	
	Mean of Means				Mean of Means			
	5.0	5.0	5.0		40.6	40.5	41.8	

table for each speaker were obtained by adding his single speech *durations* in each period and dividing this sum by his total *number of units* of talk for that period.

As is evident in Table 4.1, for *Interviewee 1,* the interviewer, aiming for a 5–5–5-second sequence, averaged 5.0, 5.3, and 5.0 seconds of speech per utterance in these three periods, respectively. He was answered by Interviewee 1 with utterances of average lengths of 17.6, 15.6, and 13.5 seconds, respectively. As is shown at the bottom of Table 4.1, with all 20 interviewees considered as a group, the interviewer achieved *grand* means of exactly 5.0, 5.0, and 5.0 seconds; while for the 20 interviewees, the *grand* means were 40.6, 40.5, and 41.8 seconds. Statistical analysis of these results indicates that as the interviewer did *not* vary his interperiod speech behavior with this control group of 20 interviewees the typical interviewee, in turn, showed a marked *stability* in his period-to-period durations of utterance.[2] In fact, when submitted to correlational analysis, the period-to-period correlations (Pearson) of the speech behavior of each of the 20 applicants shown in Table 4.1 was .75, p of .001 (Periods 1 to 2); .76, p of .001 (Periods 2 to 3); and .74, p of .001 (Periods 1 to 3). This correlational analysis merely confirms that each individual applicant was fairly consistent (unchanging) relative to himself (relative to his Period 1 baseline) as the similarly unchanging interviewer moved the interview into Periods 2 and 3.

The *same* mean values shown in Table 4.1 have been presented in graphic form in Figure 4.1. Each applicant's mean utterance in each of the three periods is represented by a single square; the same is done for the interviewer. Although Figure 4.1 does not permit the reader to follow, as does Table 4.1, what a single applicant did in each of the three periods, it does, however, present the overall findings more conveniently. It is now possible to see that (1) although, not surprisingly, there was some slight variability in the interviewer's mean duration of utterance from applicant to applicant (a range of from approximately 4 to 6 seconds), his capacity to follow a 5–5–5-second format with the

2. The average reader should disregard the two columns labeled "p" in Table 3. They are included for the specialist-reader who may wish to relate them to discussion of an issue presented in each of our earlier studies in which the behavior of individual interviewees was examined.

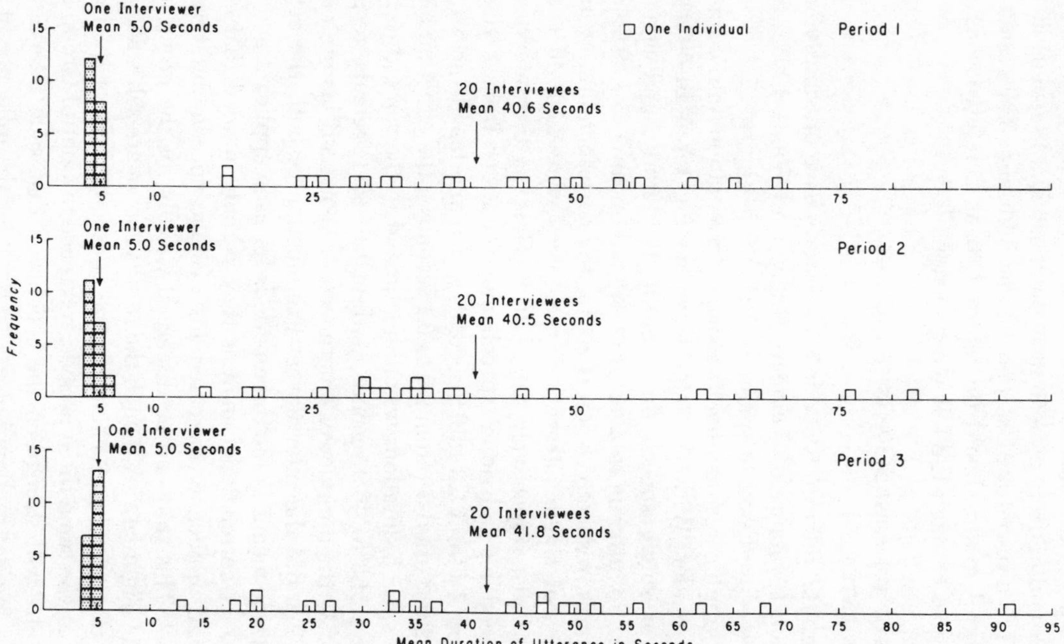

FIGURE 4.1. *Distribution of mean duration of utterances during three periods for 20 individuals, and for one interviewer (JDM). Control Group 2.*

group as a whole was demonstrated (empirically, his means were 5.0, 5.0, and 5.0 seconds with this group); and (2) the distribution of means of the individual applicants showed a *wide* range of individual variability in each of the three periods, with the range extending from a mean of approximately 13 seconds at the low end to a mean of 91 seconds at the high end. The results in this control group should be referred to as a reference as the reader goes through the following section.

RESULTS OF THE FIRST 5–10–5 STUDY: CHANGE IS DEMONSTRATED

Although the full results of our 5–10–5 study have previously been published (Matarazzo, Weitman, Saslow, and Wiens, 1963), they are here reproduced in summary fashion in Figure 4.2.

The graphic results should make interpretation fairly simple for the reader. With the interviewer aiming for 5–10–5-second means of single speech durations in this study, and actually speaking in utterances averaging (grand means) 5.3, 9.9, and 6.1 seconds, respectively (p of .001), the corresponding average durations of single interviewee utterances were 24.3, 46.9, and 26.6 seconds, respectively (p of .01). Thus, as the interviewer lengthened his individual speech unit durations from Period 1 to Period 2 (from 5.3 to 9.9 seconds), and shortened them from Period 2 to Period 3 (from 9.9 to 6.1 seconds), the effect on interviewee speech durations was dramatic and in the same direction (namely, 24.3 to 46.9 seconds, and 46.9 to 26.6 seconds, respectively). As the interviewer lengthened or shortened his utterance lengths, so did the interviewee! Examination of both the actual interviewee means in the three periods for each applicant and the more exact correlational analysis they permit revealed that *each* of the 20 applicants increased his average speech duration in Period 2. This shift can be discerned visually for the group as a whole in Figure 4.2. Although the results shown are self-sufficient, in that the interviewee changes parallel exactly those of the interviewer in the same three periods, reference to Control Group 2 in Figure 4.1 will strengthen the conclusion that such interviewee changes are *not* random but are truly under the influence of the interviewer.

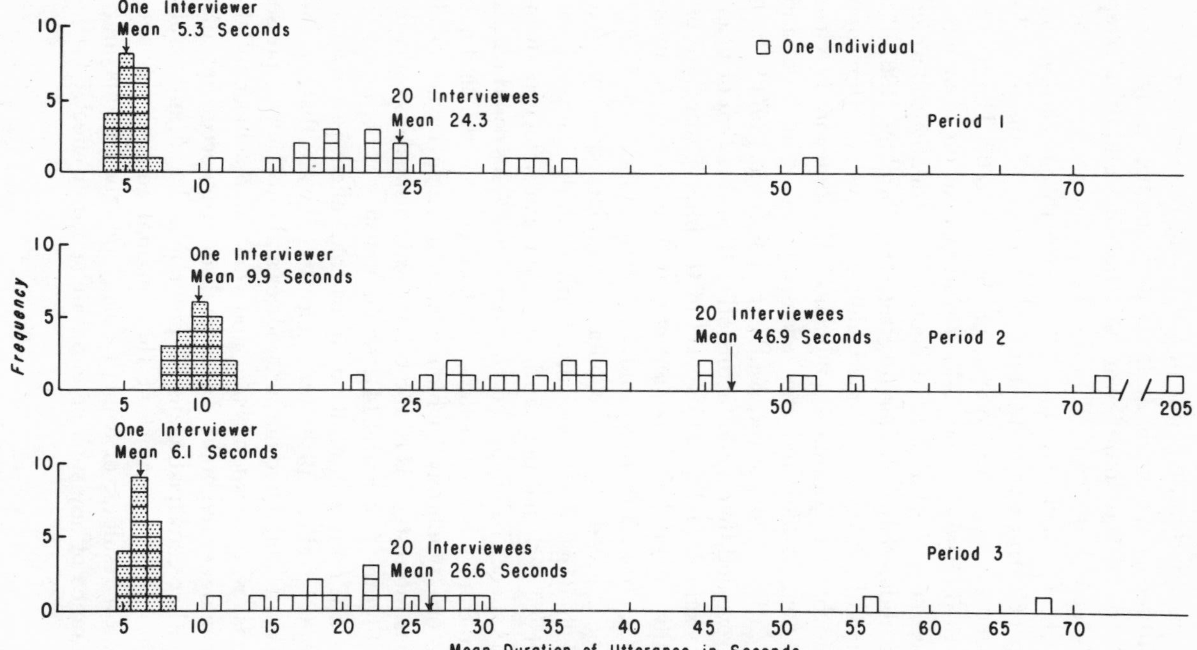

FIGURE 4.2. *Distribution of mean duration of utterances during 3 periods for 20 individuals, and for one interviewer.*

To further our understanding of this phenomenon we next designed and carried out two related studies: one utilizing the same interviewer durations but in a different sequence or order (a 10–5–10-second research design); and another designed to test the limits of this interviewer influence one additional step (a 5–15–5-second design). The results, equally clear-cut, are shown in the top half of Figure 4.3 along with our *earlier* control group (Control Group 1). Fuller discussion of these results can be found in Matarazzo, Wiens, and Saslow, 1965. The results of our 5–10–5, 10–5–10, and 5–15–5 studies take on even more significance now that they have been independently confirmed and crossvalidated by another investigator (Simpkins, 1967) in a slight modification of our methodology. However, the *complexity* of the susceptibility-to-influence phenomenon is clear from our own studies and the recent studies of Jackson and Pepinsky (1972) and Lauver, Kelley, and Froehle (1971), both of which revealed that when factors other than duration of utterance (for example, RTL, status level of the interviewer) are experimentally manipulated *concurrently* with a change in interviewer DOU from 5 to 10 seconds, the finding shown in Figure 4.2 may be masked. We have obtained similar but as yet unpublished findings. Parenthetically, in their study Lauver et al. imply that we feel that only an interviewer can influence an interviewee's speech behavior and not the reverse. This could hardly be further from our own belief—a fact clear from the findings, especially on "synchrony," which will soon be reviewed. Such influence as interests us is reciprocal across two speakers (see, for example, Figures 4.11 and 4.14). As an amusing aside, however, one might ask Lauver et al, if an "instructed" client isn't now an "interviewer?" Heller (1968, 1971) clearly is aware that we are talking about E and S and not interviewer and interviewee, per se. The issue is: who is experimenter and who naive subject in laboratory analogue research? In naturalistic free-occurring dialogues, neither conversationalist is programmed and any resulting synchrony is a product of their natural mutual influence rather than a resultant of a methodology designed to maximize the appearance of any such potential influence or effect.

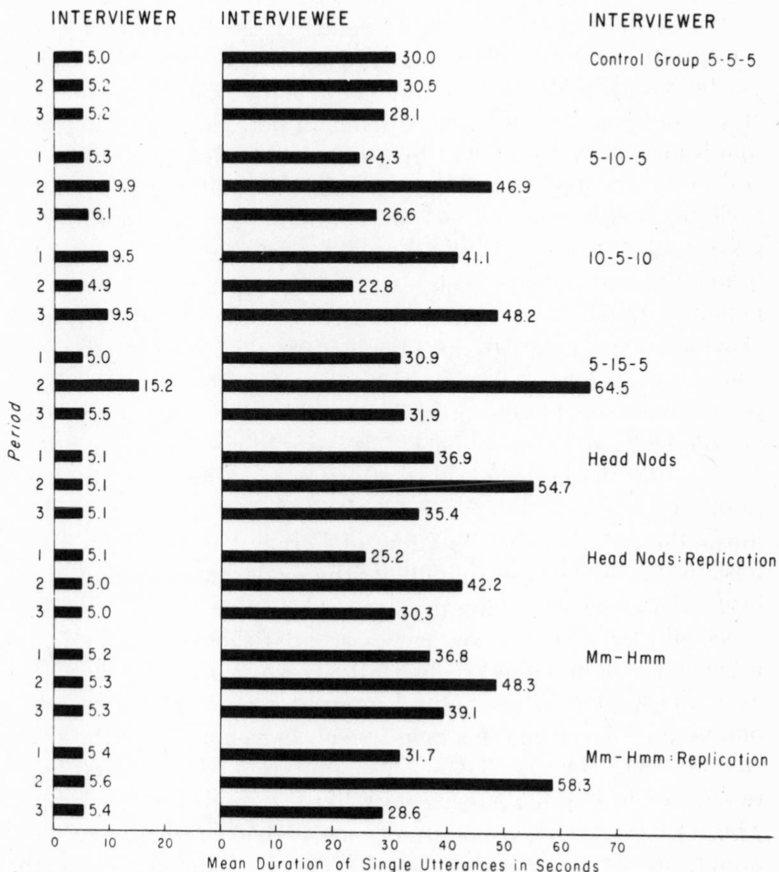

FIGURE 4.3. *Interviewer influence on duration of interviewee speech.*

ADDITIONAL INTERVIEWER TACTICS THAT MODIFY UTTERANCE LENGTH.

The actual format or research design of the additional studies summarized in the bottom half of Figure 4.3 is probably clear to the reader. In the two "Head Nod" studies the interviewer interviewed each applicant exactly as he did in the two control group studies (by utilizing a 5–5–5-second utterance schedule), except that in Period 2 the interviewer *nodded* his head each time the applicant began to talk and did so again periodically during each such interviewee utterance. In the two "Mm-hmm" studies also shown, the same research design was followed except that the interviewer substituted a periodic verbal "Mm-hmm, mm-hmm" for the head nodding of the former two studies.

The various results make relative interpretation somewhat cumbersome since the Period 1 "baseline" values for the 20 interviewees in the eight groups shown vary slightly from study to study. To overcome this problem, and thus to allow study-to-study comparisons, the interviewee values for each group were *converted to a common base.* This was done, for each group, by dividing the mean duration of utterance value in each of the three periods by the Period 1 value in that same study. This arithmetically converts the value of Period 1 to unity (1.00) in each of the eight groups and allows the reader to compare directly each of the two remaining periods to this value of unity and also to make direct similar comparisons across each study. The converted mean interviewee values are shown in Figure 4.4.

It is clear that, in the control group, for example, as the interviewer did *not* change his own speech behavior across the three periods (5.0, 5.2, and 5.2; p not significant), the average duration of speech of his interviewees likewise remained unchanged (1.00, 1.02, and .94; p not significant). That is, they were close in this speech characteristic to the Period 1 unity value in the two subsequent periods (1.02 and .94).

The 5–10–5 study also can now be interpreted in the same manner: as the interviewer lengthened and shortened his own single speech durations, the interviewees did likewise (a change from 1.00 to 1.93 and back to 1.09, respectively). These results

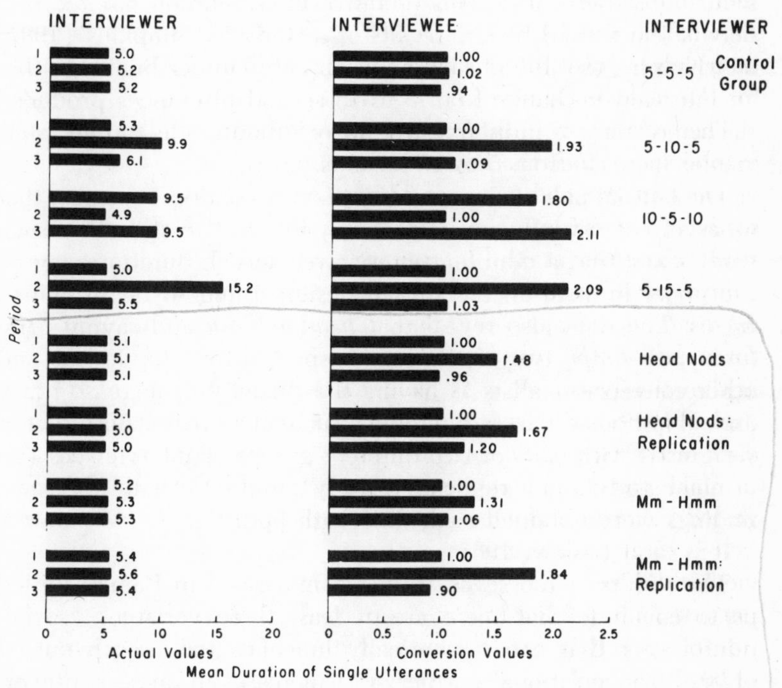

FIGURE 4.4. *Interviewer influence on duration of interviewee speech (converted to a common base).*

are confirmed in the 10–5–10 study (1.80 to 1.00 to 2.11, respectively). Interestingly, in the 5–15–5 study, a *threefold* increase in the interviewer's own duration of utterance (5.0, 15.2, and 5.5 seconds), produced only a *two-fold* increase in the average length of utterance of his conversational partners (1.00, 2.09, and 1.03). We earlier interpreted this tentatively as suggesting that there quite probably is an *upper limit* to how much one speaker can induce change in the speech behavior of his conversational partner, and that *upper limit* probably averages out to be twofold. At least this appears the case under the conditions obtaining in the studies just described. This tentative interpretation has recently been strengthened by the results of a study by Simpkins (1967) in which he, too, found such an asymptote (upper limit), in that an interviewer change from 5 to 15 second utterances produced the same increase in interviewee speech duration as did an interviewer increase from 5 to 10 seconds.

The bottom half of Figure 4.4 appears to confirm our guess that an asymptote of influence is probably inherent in still other such studies and that a doubling interviewee speech duration may be the upper limit in all the studies designed and so far examined by us. The data also reveal that *headnodding* and saying *Mm-hmm, mm-hmm,* two tactics long suspected by interviewers and other conversationalists as having the capacity to increase utterance durations do, in fact, produce such an increase. Both tactics were used with each of two different groups of interviewees (an original study and a replication study), and essentially the same findings were obtained each time with both tactics (Matarazzo, Wiens, and Saslow, 1965).

The results of the seven studies summarized in Figure 4.4 led us to conclude that there are at least three variables (social-reinforcers) that can dramatically influence the speech output of one's conversational partner: (1) increases in one's own average unit speech duration; (2) nodding one's head; and (3) saying *Mm-hmm, mm-hmm.* In our more detailed reports of these studies we have speculated that these three tactics all may have in common that they represent *greater activity,* or more "human output," in the sense of greater involvement on the part of the interviewer, thus suggesting to his conversational partner that the interviewer is *more interested in him.* The hypothesized resulting state of *greater satisfaction* produced in the interviewee-partner may be the motivating force that produces the stimulus for the latter's longer average unit speech durations in the presence of these three tactics. We are carrying out a series of additional studies designed to examine more explicitly and directly this "greater-satisfaction-in-the-presence-of-greater-interviewer-activity" hypothesis.

DURATION OF UTTERANCE: TWO NOVEL APPLICATIONS.

The findings in the top half of Figures 4.3 and 4.4 reveal that under the quasi-controlled laboratory conditions of a three-period standardized, albeit spontaneous-appearing employment interview, planned increases in the unit speech duration of one speaker are associated with corresponding increases in the unit speech duration of the second speaker. We have had the unusual opportunity of seeing this finding tested in two situations far removed from such laboratory experimentation.

The first situation arose in conjunction with America's manned space program. We were able to record the ground-to-capsule conversation between our first orbital astronaut, John Glenn, as he made his epic three-orbit flight (Matarazzo, Wiens, Saslow, Dunham, and Voas, 1964). Analysis of the utterance-by-utterance conversation between him and the 14 different ground communicators who were stationed around the globe permitted us to compute a mean duration per utterance for the astronaut and also for the combined group of ground communicators for each of the three orbits. The results are shown in Figure 4.5. The ground communicators' average durations of speech during the three orbits were 4.0, 3.9, and 3.8 seconds, respectively, while the corresponding astronaut utterance averaged 6.8, 6.5, and 4.6 seconds, respectively. The correspondence in the relative lengths of the two sets of utterances was perfect! To check this finding further we conducted a similar analysis of the ground-to-capsule speech behavior of America's second orbital astronaut, Scott Carpenter. These results, also shown in Figure 4.5, showed a perfect correspondence in the relative lengths of the speech durations of both communicators (ground and astronaut). Our conclusion from

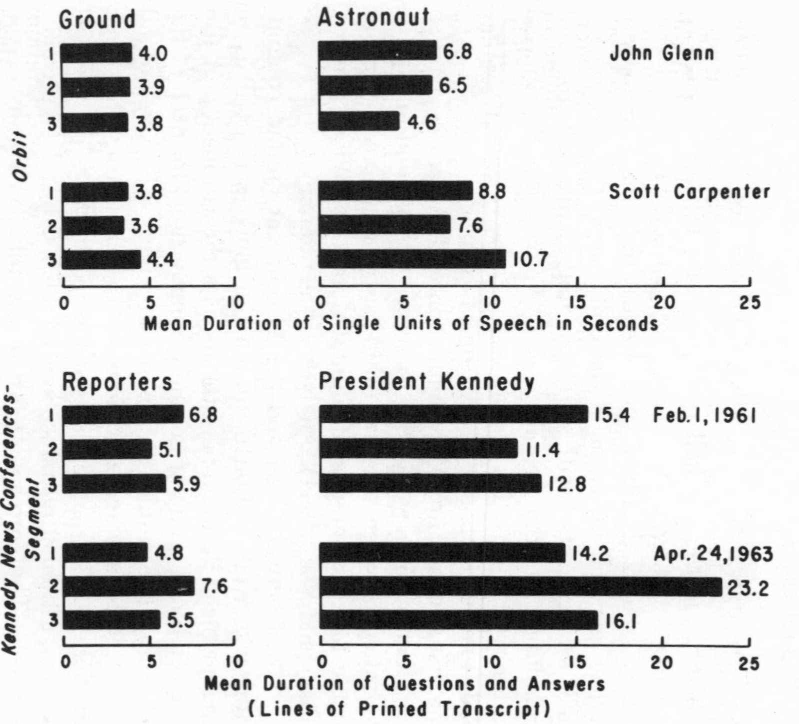

FIGURE 4.5. *Duration of utterance: two applications.*

this unplanned, nonlaboratory "experiment of nature" was that the quasi-laboratory findings shown in Figures 4.3 and 4.4 also appeared to hold under three further conditions: (1) in an unplanned and therefore "natural" setting, (2) in a situation wherein the two speakers were separated by many miles, rather than talking face to face, and (3) in a situation where one end of the conversational dyad consisted of 14 different speakers and the other end consisted of only one speaker.

A novel extension of this finding with the astronauts, also involving multiple speakers at one end of the otherwise "face-to-face" dyad, was published shortly thereafter by Ray and Webb (1966). Reasoning from our laboratory and astronaut duration of utterance findings, Ray and Webb predicted that the speech behavior of President Kennedy and the multiple reporters interviewing him might show a concordance not unlike that found in the astronaut study. Their results showed just this. For their data they obtained the published complete transcripts of 61 regular Kennedy news conferences held during his presidency. In view of their historical importance these presidential news conferences had been transcribed with unusual accuracy and fidelity. Reasoning from one of our earlier findings, since published by Matarazzo, Holman, and Wiens (1967), that the *number of words* in an utterance, obtained by a simple word count, is almost a perfect measure of the *duration* of that same utterance in seconds as this is obtained by recording devices such as the Interaction Recorder, Ray and Webb counted the number of lines of words in each question posed by a reporter and the number of lines of words in President Kennedy's reply for each of the 61 news conferences.

Their main conclusion was based on a systematic statistical evaluation of their results. However, to make the visual presentatation of their results similar to our three-orbit astronaut figure, they divided each news conference into thirds. Two examples of their main finding, illustrative of their major findings, provide a striking overall confirmation of our astronaut results and are given in the bottom half of Figure 4.5. The concordance is perfect. (We have described all the results shown in Figure 4.5 by the term "concordance" since, unlike the laboratory findings shown in Figures

4.3 and 4.4, we cannot be sure which member of the dyad is influencing whom. It may very well be, as our later psychotherapy results will suggest, that the influence is mutual.)

In any event, the astronaut and presidential news conference findings may suggest to the reader a number of other nonlaboratory natural settings in which to test the implications of more formal findings. The astronaut and President Kennedy data along with Simpkins' (1967) independent confirmation of our 5–10–5 and 5–15–5 results lead us to conclude that duration of utterance is a variable clearly influenced by the duration of utterance of one's conversational partner.

Reaction Time Latency: Modifiability Studies

After completing these studies, we spent the major portion of the next years investigating whether the reaction time latency variable in interviewee speech behavior could be similarly influenced by planned changes in the latency behavior of the interviewer. The reaction time latency (RTL) data in Figure 4.6 (not previously published), come from the same (second) control group whose mean utterance durations are plotted in Figure 4.1. With this group of 20 applicants the interviewer had been instructed *not* to vary, across the three periods, either his utterance lengths (these followed a 5–5–5-second design) or his reaction time latencies. This latter reaction time latency schedule followed a 1–1–1-second design in that the interviewer was instructed to answer (with a 5-second utterance) each completed applicant comment with a reaction time of *less than one second.* That the interviewer followed his instructions is clear from his actual mean reaction time latencies in the three periods. These were .43, .44, and .46 seconds, respectively. Examination of each of the 20 individual means for the interviewer indicates that with each applicant he did, in fact, answer following a pause lasting less than one second.

The right-hand side of Figure 4.6 shows the corresponding RTL of the 20 applicants. As the interviewer maintained a steady RTL (.43, .44, and .46 seconds; *p* not significant), they answered him with an unchanging mean RTL (.99–.89–.91 seconds; *p* not sig-

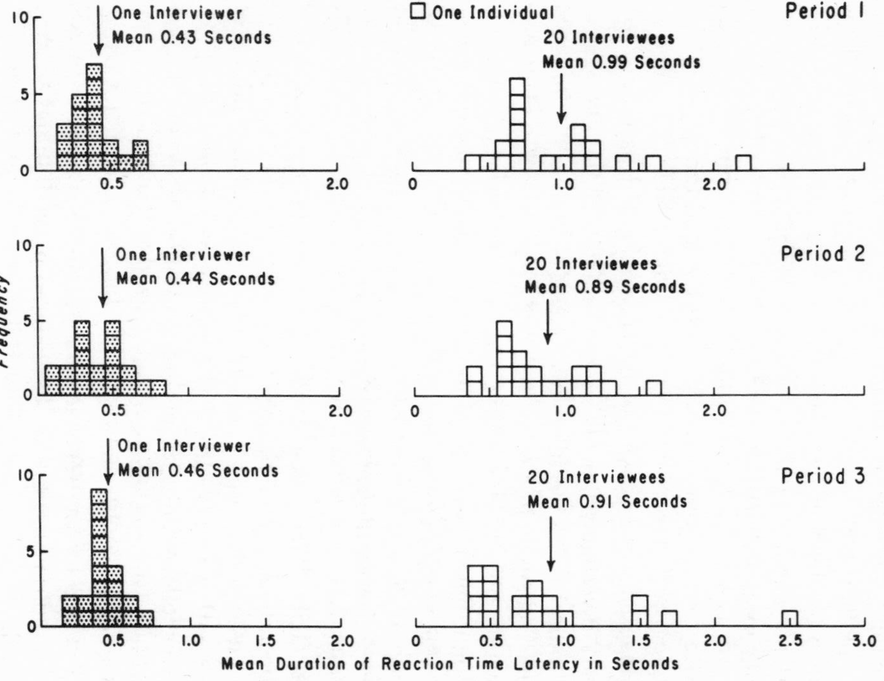

FIGURE 4.6. *Distribution of mean duration of reaction time latency during three periods for 20 individuals, and for one interviewer (JDM). Control Group 2.*

nificant). In addition, and once again, one sees clear evidence of wide *individual differences* (in RTL) from one applicant to another, although the lock-step concordance in RTL for each applicant relative to his own Period 1 baseline obtained here also. The period-to-period correlations in RTL for the 20 individual applicants were: Period 1 to 2, *r* of .57 (*p* of .01); Period 2 to 3, *r* of .30 (*p* not significant); and Period 1 to 3, *r* of .64 (*p* of .01). For the comparable periods shown in Figure 4.7, these same three values of Pearson *r* for the 20 applicants are .63 (*p* of .01), .72 (*p* of .001), and .74 (*p* of .001), respectively.

The results shown in Figure 4.6 lead to these conclusions: an interviewer can faithfully program himself to interview spontaneously with reaction time latencies of 1–1–1, and the effect of this unchanging behavior on his part is a similar lack of change in the average latency behavior of his conversational partner.

In the next group we studied, we programmed the interviewer to follow a 1–5–1 reaction time latency schedule; this was followed by additional studies in which he was asked to follow RTL schedules of 5–1–5 seconds, 1–10–1 seconds, and finally 1–15–1 seconds. (Only the results of the 1–5–1 and 5–1–5 studies have been published previously [Matarazzo and Wiens, 1967]). Accordingly, Figures 4.7 and 4.8 contain these previously unpublished results of the 1–10–1 study and the 1–15–1 study. Figure 4.7 reveals that, as the interviewer varied his own mean RTL (.54, 10.16, and .62 seconds; *p* of .001), the RTL of the interviewees followed him faithfully (.93, 1.62, and .87 seconds; *p* of .001). The comparable mean values in Figure 4.8 are .50, 14.86, and .51 seconds; *p* of .001, and 1.04, 1.75, and 1.10 seconds; *p* of .001, respectively.

The results of these two studies, as well as those of the previously published studies, are summarized at the top of Figure 4.9. The control group shown at the top is the earlier Control Group 1, previously reported with the 1–5–1 and 5–1–5 studies, and is not Control Group 2 (here reported for the first time in Figure 4.6). The last three studies shown relate to a somewhat different issue and will not be discussed in this section.

To permit, once again, direct study-to-study comparisons, the RTL data in Figure 4.9 were converted into values with a base of unity by a method comparable to the one discussed in relation

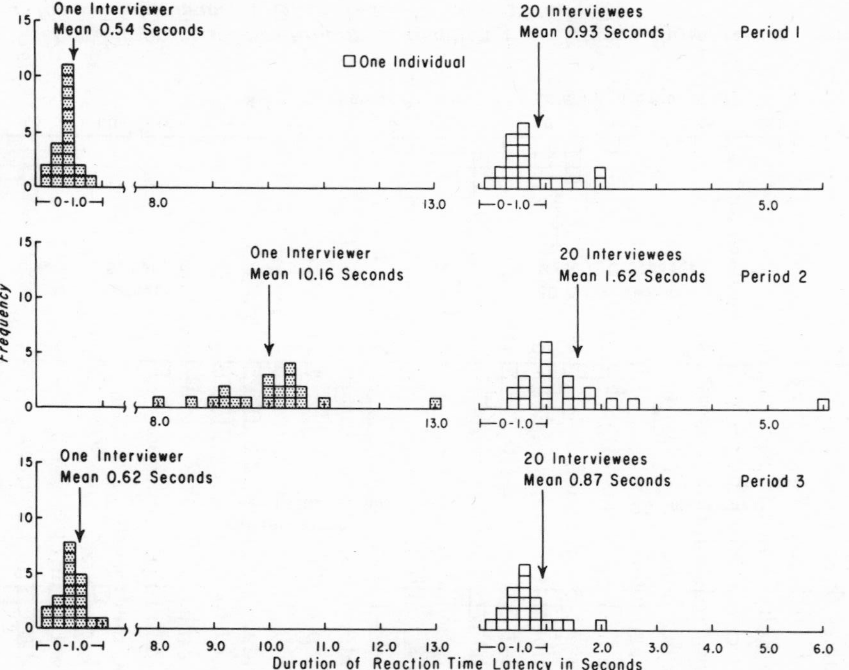

FIGURE 4.7. *Distribution of mean duration of reaction time latency during three periods for 20 individuals and for one interviewer (JDM).*

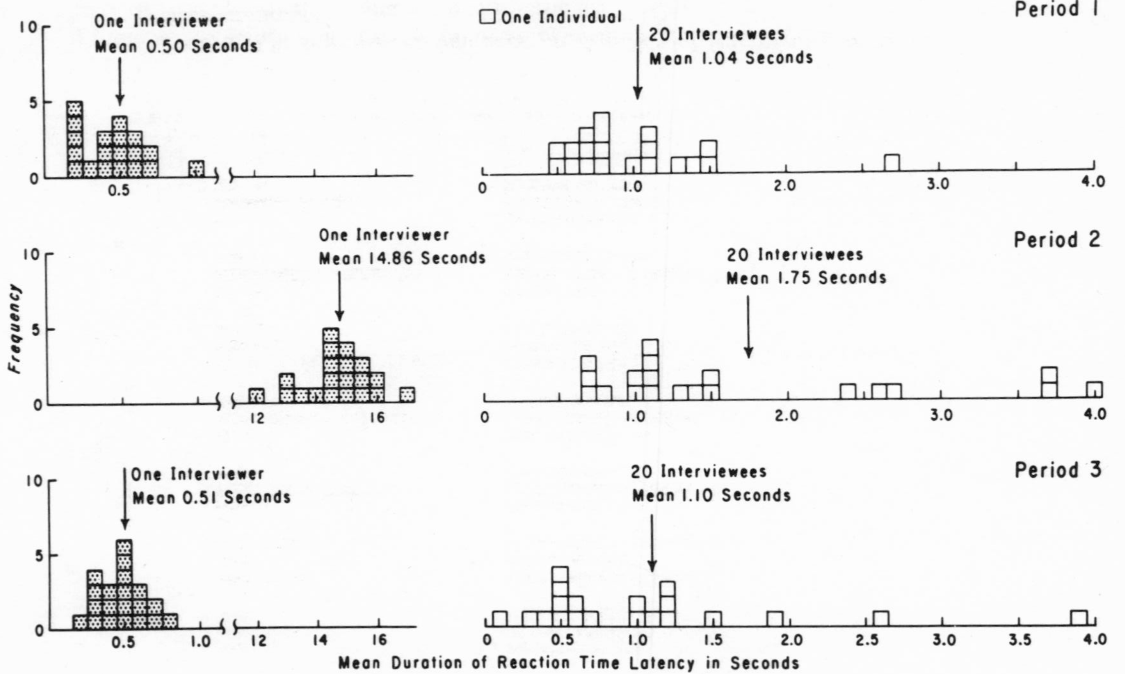

FIGURE 4.8. *Distribution of mean duration of reaction time latency during three periods for 20 individuals and for one interviewer (JDM). 1–15–1 Latency Study.*

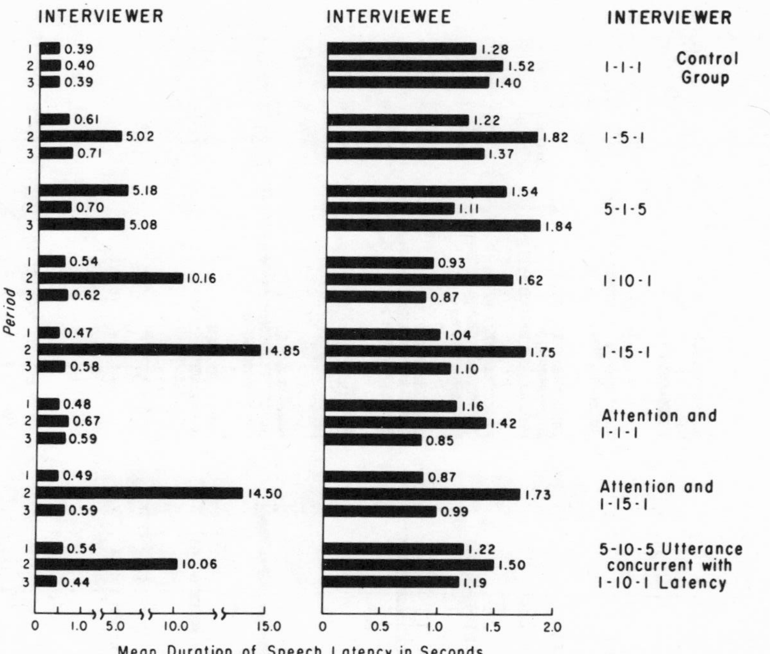

FIGURE 4.9. *Interviewer influence on duration of interviewee reaction time latencies.*

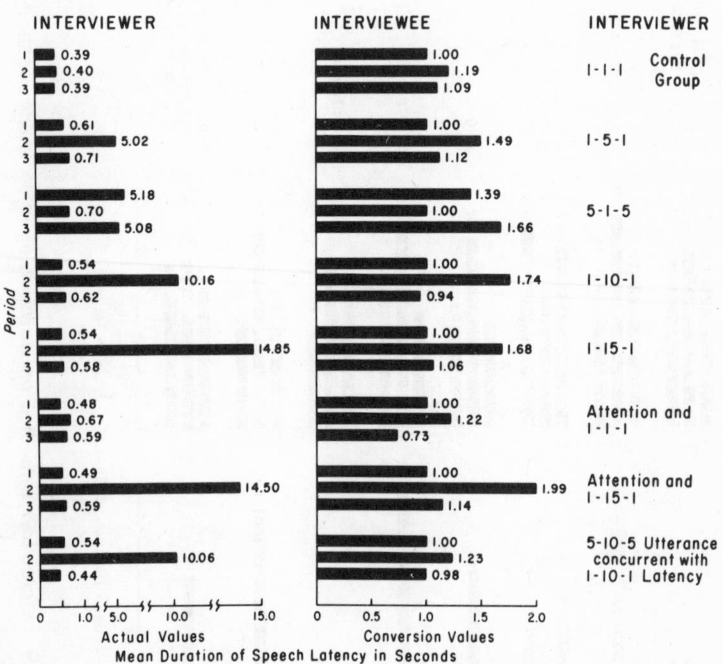

FIGURE 4.10. *Interviewer influence on duration of interviewee reaction time latencies (converted to a common base).*

to Figure 4.4. These converted values for the reaction time latency studies are shown in Figure 4.10. Inspection of this figure reveals that *each* of the scheduled interviewer *increases* in his own RTL (be they increases from 1 second to 5, or 1 to 10, or 1 to 15 seconds) produced a corresponding *increase* in the reaction time latency of his respondents. Likewise, decreases in his own RTL were faithfully mirrored by the applicants. These changes reached high levels of statistical significance and were present in each of the four studies, thus leaving no question that a variable (socially-reinforcing behavioral change) has been discovered that can increase or decrease the speed (latency) of response from a conversational partner: the simple tactic of increasing or decreasing the average speed with which the first speaker answers him. The recent confirmation of this RTL susceptibility-to-influence-finding by Jackson and Pepinsky (1972) in a study comparable to our 1–10–1 study in Figure 4.10 adds to our belief in the viability of this finding. However their study was more complex than simply a 1–10–1 RTL study and had some features in common with the study summarized at the bottom of the figure.

The results permit a conclusion beyond the one that an increase in one speaker's RTL will be associated with a concomitant increase in the other speaker's RTL. As with the duration of utterance variable presented in Figure 4.4, in these quasi-laboratory studies there appears to be an *upper limit* to this potential influence on RTL. An interviewer in this situation apparently can induce a change of roughly 50 to 70 percent in his respondent's average time of response, and this asymptote appears whether the first speaker changes his own latency behavior from one second to five seconds or doubles the change to 10 seconds, or triples it to 15 seconds!

Americans appear to vary very little in the quickness of speed with which they respond (RTL) to their conversational partners under most social circumstances. The applicant data shown in Figures 4.6, 4.7, and 4.8 reveal that, in fact, each of these individual 60 young men spoke with an average RTL that varied only slightly around the group means shown. In social, or quasi-social conversations most of us probably answer our conversational partner in less than two seconds. The recently published data of Jaffe and Feldstein (1970, p. 76) with normals in dialogue show just that. It is probably because such an individualized "tempo" (RTL) is practiced by each of us hundreds of times daily that greater changes than those shown in Figure 4.10 could not be induced by the interviewer. Nevertheless, given the narrow range within which RTL expresses itself in most of us, the 50 to 70 percent increase demonstrated is undoubtedly a finding of considerable potential importance. One need only imagine for a moment the possible implications of the results shown in Figure 4.10 for such potential applications as, through *planned* practice sessions with a programmed "instructor," (1) helping shy young boys and girls and men and women to be less "tongue-tied" in everyday social conversation, (2) getting husbands and wives who find each other's verbal tempos burdensome to become better synchronized, (3) helping novice-psychotherapists and other student-interviewers to learn how to wait longer before answering their interviewee. Many similar potential applications of the DOU results shown in Figure 4.4 will also occur to the reader, especially as these might apply in such important person-to-person situations as those found in the home, classroom, and other important settings. Some implications of these findings for the psychotherapy situation were described in a previous publication (Matarazzo, 1962).

REACTION TIME LATENCY: ONE APPLICATION

A recently completed study of speech and silence behavior in the clinical psychotherapy situation (Matarazzo, Wiens, Matarazzo, and Saslow, 1968) allowed us an opportunity to examine, in this less structured, quasi-natural clinical setting, the potential application of the RTL results summarized in Figures 4.9 and 4.10. The study analyzed, for each psychotherapy session conducted, the unit-by-unit verbal exchanges of seven patients with their respective individual psychotherapist throughout the whole of each psychotherapy. One aspect of the study compared the mean reaction time latency of each of the two participants in *each* of their clinical sessions. Plotting these session-to-session pairs of means permitted us the opportunity to examine for evidence of possible synchrony, or concordance, in the relationship between the RTL of one member of the dyad and the RTL of the other on the same day (session).

The results with one of the seven patient-therapist pairs are presented in Figure 4.11. The patient is SM, an 18-year-old girl who was hospitalized for depression and attempted suicide. Her therapist is Ruth G. Matarazzo (RGM), an experienced psychologist. They met for 20 sessions of clinical psychotherapy, during which the therapist and patient behaved "naturally." That is, unlike the interviewer (who was programmed to vary his reaction time latencies according to prescribed schedules), in the studies summarized in Figures 4.9 and 4.10, therapist RGM was merely asked to behave in the therapy sessions as she would in any other clinical psychotherapy. Each of the therapists in this study reported it was quite easy for them to behave naturally after the first one or two observational recordings.

The illustrative result shown in Figure 4.11 is similar to that found in the other psychotherapy pairs: there is present a rather clear evidence of synchrony between the reaction time latency behavior of the two participants. The statistical index of this association, a Pearson correlation of .60, is highly significant (*p* of .01). As the patient's reaction time before speaking increased in one session or decreased in a subsequent session, the reaction time of the therapist followed or "modeled" it perfectly, and vice versa. The finding of such synchrony, as well as that found in the remaining sets of patient-therapist pairs, provides strong evidence that the results from the more experimentally controlled studies summarized for the reaction time latency variable in Figures 4.9 and 4.10 will quite likely be duplicated and crossvalidated in a number of other more natural settings. Jaffe and Feldstein (1970, p. 45) report one such crossvalidation of synchrony in the silence behavior of pairs of conversationalists. (Interestingly, they also report a finding similar to ours of an absence of such synchrony in the utterance length behavior of the two conversationalists.) We hope that social and other behavioral scientists will be stimulated by these findings to look for additional examples of such synchrony. For example, will such synchrony or modeling be even stronger in pairs of individuals who like each other? Will it be weaker, absent, or negative in direction in people who dislike

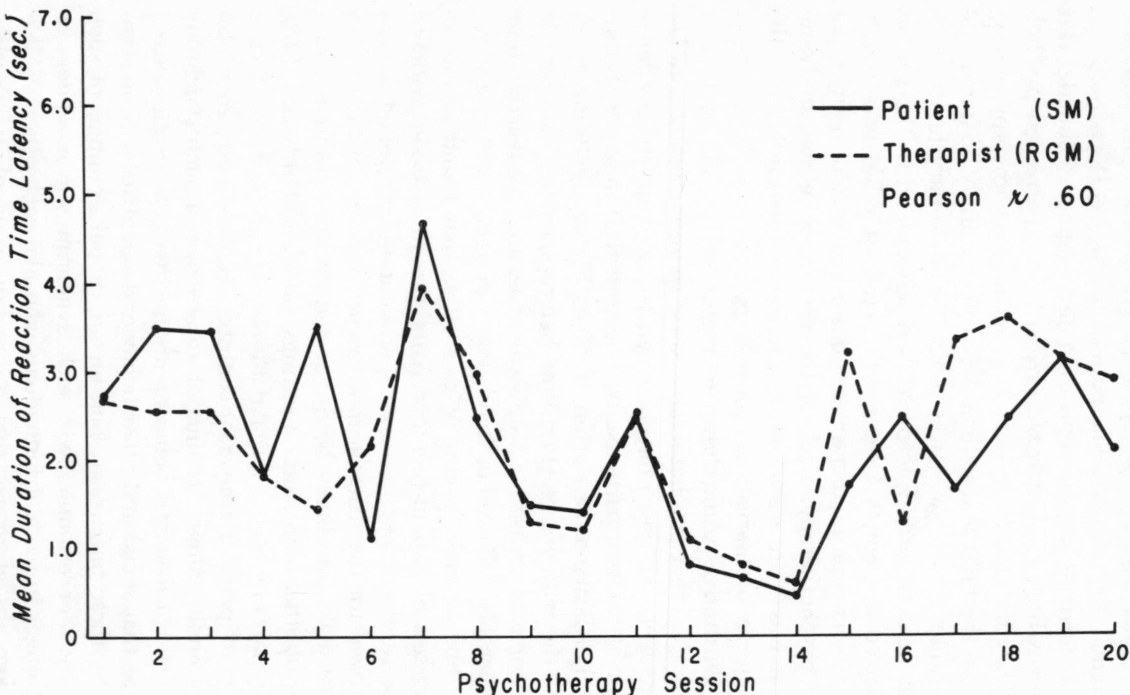

FIGURE 4.11. *Mean reaction time latency over sessions.*

each other? How will it show itself in parent-child relationships of different qualities? Or in the early, middle (so-called "transference"), and last stages of psychotherapy? Or in psychotherapeutic and other conversational samples where there is more (or less) "empathy" being evidenced? The potential researchable questions would appear to be endless.

Interruption: Modifiability Studies

In a previous report (Wiens, Saslow, and Matarazzo, 1966) we presented *incidental* findings from study of the 99 patients discussed earlier that indicated that the amount of interrupting one speaker does of a second speaker can be modified by increasing or decreasing the extent of this behavior in one of the two speakers. We subsequently completed a study not previously published *explicitly designed* to experimentally vary the amount of interrupting behavior of the interviewer in order to examine the effect of this tactic on the interruption behavior of the interviewee. The results were compared with those in a control group.

Figure 4.12 shows the extent to which 20 applicants interrupted the interviewer when the latter was programmed *not* to interrupt them. The data are from Control Group 2, which was previously described. The data are presented for each applicant in the form of a percentage that characterizes what percent of his total number of utterances in each period consisted of an interruption of the interviewer. Since different applicants spoke different numbers of times in each of the periods, converting each person's units of interruption to a percentage of his own total units of utterances makes the data from individual to individual readily comparable.

The interviewer followed his instructions and "interrupted" according to an 0–0–0 "interruption schedule" across the three periods. The natural (baseline) response from the applicants to such a noninterrupting stimulus input appears to be a 10 percent applicant rate of interruption; more specifically, their percentage interruptions across the three periods of this control interview were 8.5, 9.8, and 11.2 (p is not significant), respectively. These percentages are consistent with the grand mean (of 9.2 percent)

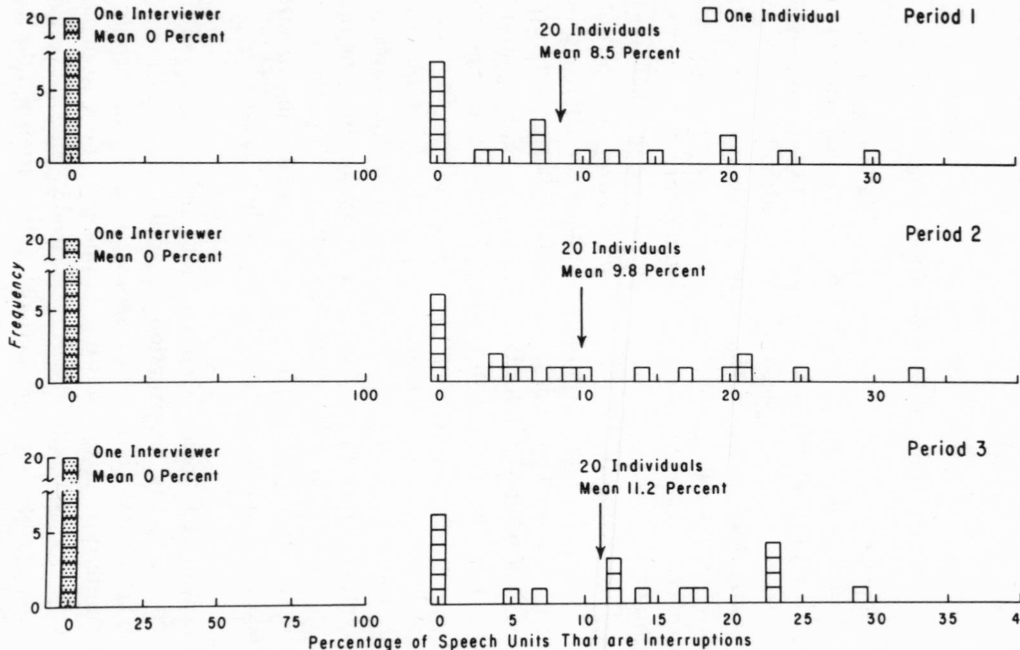

FIGURE 4.12. *Frequency distribution: percentage of all interviewee speech units that are interruptions of the interviewer (JDM). Control Group 2.*

of such interruption rates from the 10 additional studies summarized at the bottom of Figure 2.15. This value suggests that in the presence of a noninterrupting interviewer, the average applicant interrupts the interviewer about one time in each block of 10 utterances he, the applicant, emits. The previously discussed Figure 2.15 reveals that such a one-in-ten rate holds over a variety of other interviewer-programmed input conditions, providing, of course, that *none* of these other conditions is an interrupting instruction to the interviewer (the case with all 10 studies shown in Figure 2.15).

Despite the fact that the results in Figure 4.12 (as well as those in Figure 2.15) yield a fairly constant *mean* rate of interruption of 10 percent, it also is obvious from Figure 4.12 that there are wide *individual differences* in this rate of interruption from applicant to applicant. Thus, at the low end in Period 1, seven of the 20 applicants showed a zero interruption rate whereas, in the same period and while exposed to a comparable stimulus input (a noninterrupting interviewer), one applicant interrupted in three out of each 10 utterances he contributed (a rate of 30 percent).

To test the extent to which the interruption rate of an interviewee could be brought under the control of the interviewer, we designed a study, again using an additional 20 applicants, wherein the interviewer was instructed to interrupt the applicant as often as he was able to do so in Period 2 while still maintaining a reasonable social decorum. We did not ask the interviewer to follow a rigid or thoroughly planned schedule of interruption. We recognized the fact that increases in interruption rate, unlike increases in DOU or RTL, can constitute a socially startling phenomenon and thereby could interfere with the much more serious social-professional responsibility of our job-selection interviewer to each applicant. Accordingly, we instructed the interviewer to interrupt as often as he felt he could within the bounds of general professional-ethical considerations and the actual situation presented by each applicant. The results, presented in Figure 4.13, indicate that, with one applicant, the interviewer interrupted 33 percent of the times he, the interviewer, spoke, whereas with an applicant at the high end, he interrupted in 92 percent of the instances in which he spoke. With this last applicant, the dynam-

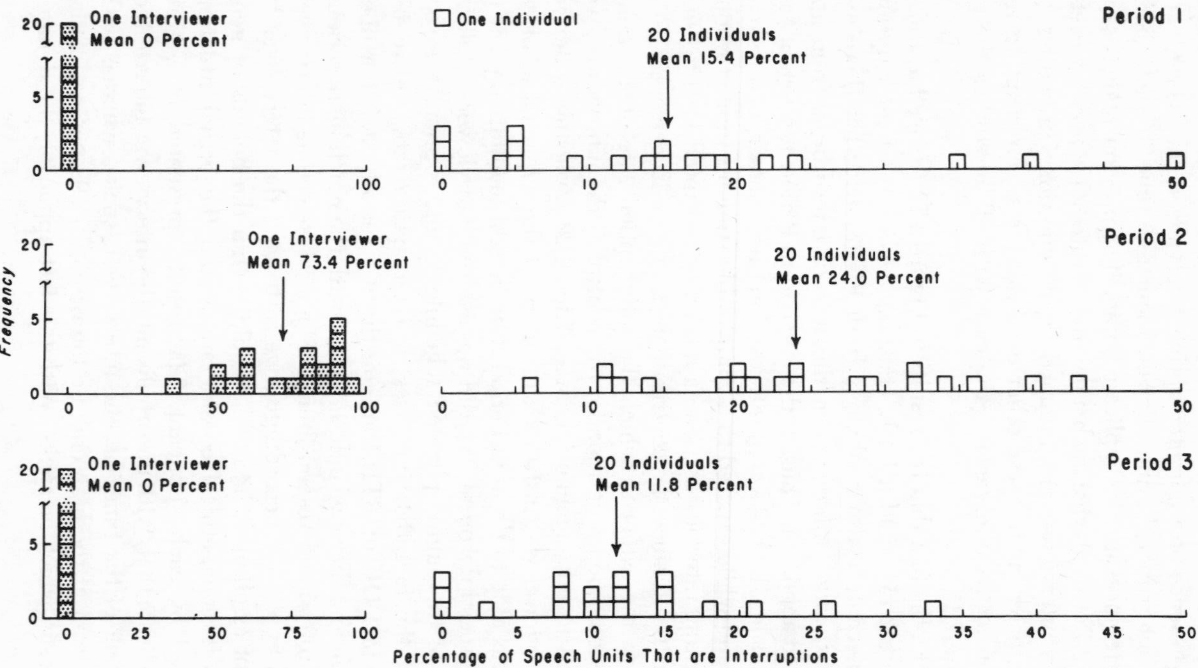

FIGURE 4.13. *Frequency distribution: percentage of all interviewee speech units that are interruptions of the interviewer (JDM). Interruption Study.*

ics of the situation made it possible for the interviewer, acting spontaneously, to interrupt almost each time he spoke in this experimental period. (As an aside, it may be necessary to mention that these interviews take place in a highly professional atmosphere, a hospital office in a medical school, and each of the studies here being summarized are fully monitored by a longstanding academic committee of professional peers set up to review such research with humans.)

The results shown on the right-hand side of Figure 4.13 present the main finding of this study. As the interviewer changed his input through a schedule of interruptions of 0.0–73.4–0.0 percent (*p* of .001), the result was a comparable increase in the average interruption rate of the applicants: 15.4–24.0–11.8 percent (*p* of .001). The "shift to the right" in Period 2 by the applicants, relative to their lower interruption levels in Periods 1 and 3, is dramatic.

The conclusion is clear: one tactic for increasing or decreasing another speaker's rate of interrupting behavior is for the second speaker to increase or decrease his own level of interrupting behavior. (However, it should be equally clear that our results merely catalog and attempt systematically to understand only one element, raw frequency or percentage of interruption, or DOU or RTL, in the rich interaction that is a dialogue. Much more, not captured by these variables, is obviously going on.)

Each of the three speech variables—duration of utterance, reaction time latency, and interruptions—can be increased or decreased by a change *in kind* from the conversational partner, and for the first two of these three variables and under the conditions of study we have used so far, there appears to be an asymptote of roughly a two-fold (100 percent) increase beyond which further increases in the interviewer's input cannot produce additional changes in the interviewee's behavior (output). The results in Figure 4.13 would suggest that such an upper limit of twice the baseline value may also hold for the interruption variable. This figure reveals that even with a massive change in the input, from a 0.0 percent interviewer interruption rate in Period 1 to a 73.4 percent interruption rate in Period 2, the net effect is, once again, less than a two-fold increase (15.4 percent to 24.0 percent). Such an increase in a behavior (interrupting) generally considered in poor taste, however, is, for this reason, probably a highly important finding.

The reader should *not* conclude that interruption rate cannot be more than doubled under any circumstances. Although it was not highlighted at the time, examination of the RGM–SM psychotherapy data in Figure 4.11 reveals a range of modifiability (increase and decrease) in the *mean reaction time latency* of roughly five to one. This is considerably more than is revealed by the less than two-to-one upper limit for change in this variable suggested by the results in Figures 4.9 and 4.10. Study of the same seven psychotherapy cases also revealed a similar wider range of modifiability for this interruption variable than is suggested in the results shown in Figure 4.13. (See one such case in Figure 4.14 below.)

INTERRUPTION: ONE APPLICATION

Study of possible synchrony in the seven psychotherapy cases with the mean *duration of utterance* variable revealed *no* such two-person concordance for this variable; despite the strength of this influence found in the seven quasi-laboratory studies on this same variable summarized in Figures 4.3 and 4.4. We have dealt at some length with various possible explanations for this lack of synchrony for DOU in another publication (Matarazzo, Wiens, Matarazzo, and Saslow, 1968). (Heller [1971, pp. 144–148] offers some additional possible reasons for our not finding a synchrony between our interviewer and interviewee speech behavior for the DOU variable.) However, in the immediately preceding section and in Figure 4.11 we reported that we *did* find synchrony in the session-to-session *reaction time latencies* of our patients and their respective psychotherapists.

For reasons not fully clear to us, the *interruption* variable showed the *greatest* degree of patient-therapist synchrony in these same seven psychotherapy cases. Figure 4.14 contains the results with one of these seven cases, RGM–SM, the same case from which the reaction time latency synchrony data of Figure 4.11 were derived. As is clear in Figure 4.14, the strength of this concordance (Pearson r of .71, p of .001), is striking and dramatic.

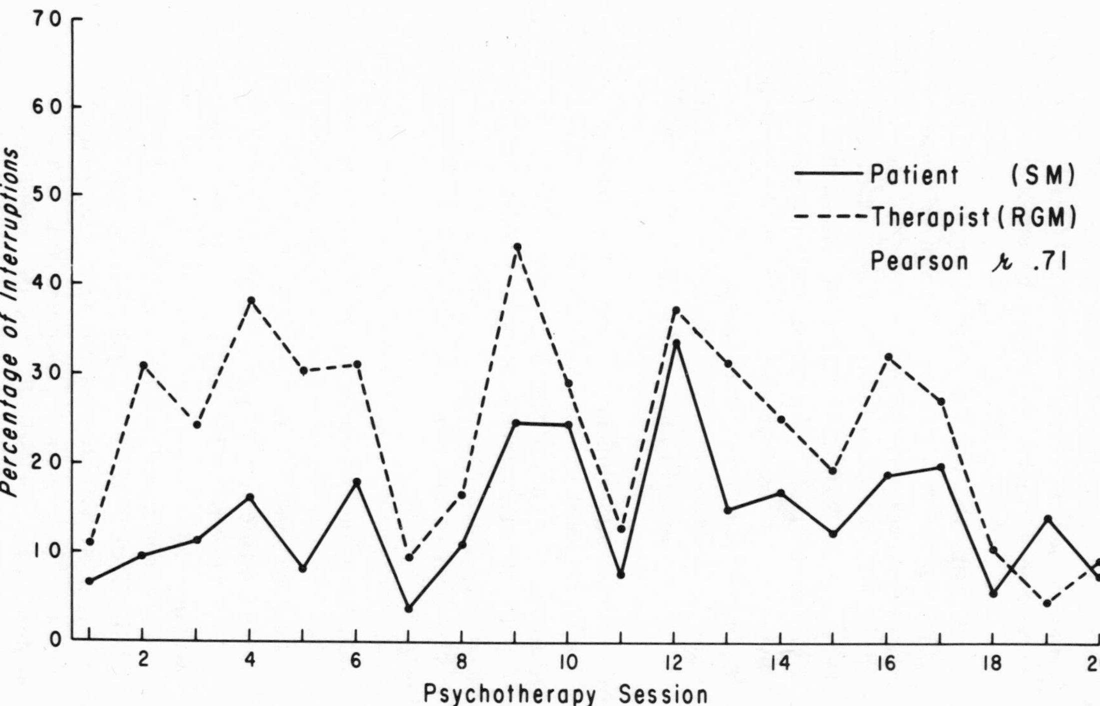

FIGURE 4.14. *Percentage of own speech units that are interruptions of the other person.*

Over the 20 psychotherapy sessions both SM and RGM showed considerable variation in the amount of interrupting they did from one session to the next. Yet, interestingly, their individual rates on any given day and their movements up and down almost perfectly mirror each other! (Jaffe and Feldstein, 1970, report similar correlation in the interruption behavior of two conversational partners.)

The results with the quasi-laboratory interviews studied in Figure 4.13 suggested that such an interviewer *cannot* produce an increase or decrease in the interruption rate of the interviewee beyond a two-fold range: an increase from 15.4 to 24.0 percent and a decrease from 24.0 to 11.8 percent. The results shown in Figure 4.14 indicate that, under the special and highly emotionally involving conditions that obtain in clinical psychotherapy, increases and decreases in interrupting behavior are possible within a range exceeding five or even eight fold! An example of this is the change in SM's interruption rate in Session 7 versus Session 9.

Many scientists and clinicians interested in research on psychotherapy have postulated the operation in such a psychotherapeutic relationship of clinical variables such as "empathy," "transference," "warmth." The results shown in Figures 4.11 and 4 .14 have led us to speculate that a number of these clinical variables may be correlates of the three speech variables we have been describing.

In any event, one final observation about the interruption variable should be made. Whereas in our society interrupting behavior often has a negative implication, our research has revealed a *positive* element. Time after time after time we have observed the highest degree of spirited animation and rapport between our interviewer and his applicant when the former began the interruption segment of the interview. The data shown in Figure 4.14 also could be interpreted in a positive rather than a negative light. That is, at the present we are conceiving of interruption behavior as possibly constituting another example to the interviewee that the interviewer is interested in him or otherwise fully involved with him. Sensing this the interviewee engages in kind (steps up his own tempo of interaction, resulting in an increase in his own rate of interruption of the interviewer). This hypothesis is in need of further investigation and explication.

Modifiability: Implications for Reliability

In Chapter 3 we discussed the question of the test-retest stability, reliability, or representativeness of a small *sample* (usually 30 to 45 minutes) of an interviewee's speech behavior. In that chapter, we presented a fair degree of research evidence that a 30-minute sample, or even less, of an interviewee's duration of utterance, reaction time latency, initiative time latency, and interruption rate yields a fairly reliable index of each of these variables for him. Yet the coefficients of correlation for test-retest samples of these speech variables fall short of the value of 1.00, which would indicate perfect reliability. There may be a number of reasons why our obtained reliability values were less than perfect. The most obvious of these is that a 30-minute[3] (or shorter) sample of speech on only the small numbers of individuals represented could hardly yield the more stable results (higher correlations) typically found in larger samples of individuals and utilizing larger samples of speech (for example, means based on 10-hour speech samples for each interviewee).

While sample size, relatively speaking, undoubtedly played a role in lowering our obtained test-retest coefficients, we believe the modifiability results offer still another potential powerful explanation for these less-than-perfect empirical indexes of stability. If even within a mere three-period, 45-minute interview an individual (interviewer), using the full knowledge of the results of this research program, can dramatically increase or decrease

3. The reader should understand that the four speech variables whose test-retest correlations are shown in Table 3.1 were derived from data collected either throughout the whole interview or from only one subperiod of this same interview. Thus the correlations for the DOU and silence variables shown in Table 3.1 were derived from the full 32-minute interview; whereas the percentage initiative correlations came only from a 7.4 minute segment (Period 2) of this same interview, and the interruption correlation from the 2.7 minute segment that constituted the Period 4-interruption segments in each of the five studies (see Wiens, Saslow, and Matarazzo, 1966, Table 3, p. 156).

the baseline level of these speech variables in another individual at will, one must imagine the potential for such "random" or "unprogrammed" influence on these same interviewees by many other people during the lengthy *test-retest interval of living* of each of the patients who took part in the less reliable-appearing one-week, five-week, and eight-month studies shown in Table 3.1. The same would appear to be possible for the 15-month interval data for the nursing supervisors shown in Figures 3.1 through 3.4. Given the fact that an instructed interviewer can reproducibly modify, up or down and at will, the speech behavior of one after another of his interviewees and that as soon as he withdraws this influencing tactic the interviewees revert to their own baseline, this fact suggests that the behavioral variables being altered under his influence are, in all probability, highly stable for any given individual. The test-retest reliability results presented in Chapter 3 are a further index of this stability. Consequently, the point is merely our guess that if we obtained larger samples of our speech variables we could demonstrate even stronger test-retest correlations than those presented in Chapter 3. In the absence of changed conditions (actual or perceived) in the second interview for those individuals who showed a change in one or another speech behavior from test to retest, we would be inclined to speculate that, although random and not planned by the experimenter, such a changing interviewee may have been exposed in the test-retest interim to a highly influential individual (or other set of stimulus conditions) who unwittingly helped bring about the change seen on retest. After all, people do marry, change jobs, and in other ways change their human environment, and thus the possibilities arise for unplanned but daily recurring experiences of the type shown in the 45-minute samples in Figures 4.4, 4.10, and 4.13. However, since these variables do, in fact, have the considerable stability they were found to have, even after a 15-month interval, for example, it would appear that marriage, and other "unprogrammed" environmental (stimulus) changes influence these characteristic speech variables only in part. For the moment, at least, our studies have left no question in our minds but that the speech variables we have been studying are both highly representative and characteristic for each individual and that they can be dramatically influenced under the proper set of programmed conditions. Our laboratory analogue research to date, in contrast to our naturalistic psychotherapy recordings, has focused only on demonstration of programmed changes of a temporary nature (within a 45-minute interview). It would appear desirable to study the conditions under which such temporarily induced changes can be made more permanent for any given individual. The implications of such research findings for parents, educators, psychotherapists are obvious (Matarazzo, 1962).

5

Some Interrelationships between Speech Variables

To better enhance the experimental rigor of our research program to date we generally have studied each of our speech variables in isolation rather than attempt to experimentally vary two of these variables at one time. We have, nevertheless, from time to time examined the effect on a second variable of changes (naturally occurring or planned) in another variable, and even have planned a new series of studies designed to experimentally vary two variables concurrently. Examples of such studies are shown at the bottom of Figures 4.9 and 4.10. Since these studies are continuing, no further presentation will be made here of our preliminary findings.

Covariation of Own RTL and Own Interrupting Behavior

However, the data from the seven psychotherapy cases (Table 3.2) did provide us with a further opportunity to examine how two of our four speech variables—reaction time latency and interruptions—correlate or otherwise affect each other. The data, from one of these seven cases, RGM–SM, are presented in Figure 5.1. The scattergram on the left for patient SM was derived as follows. In the first of her 20 psychotherapy sessions SM had a mean RTL for that session of 2.76 seconds. She also interrupted the therapist during that same session in 6.7 percent of all the utterances she contributed that day. Consequently, to find the

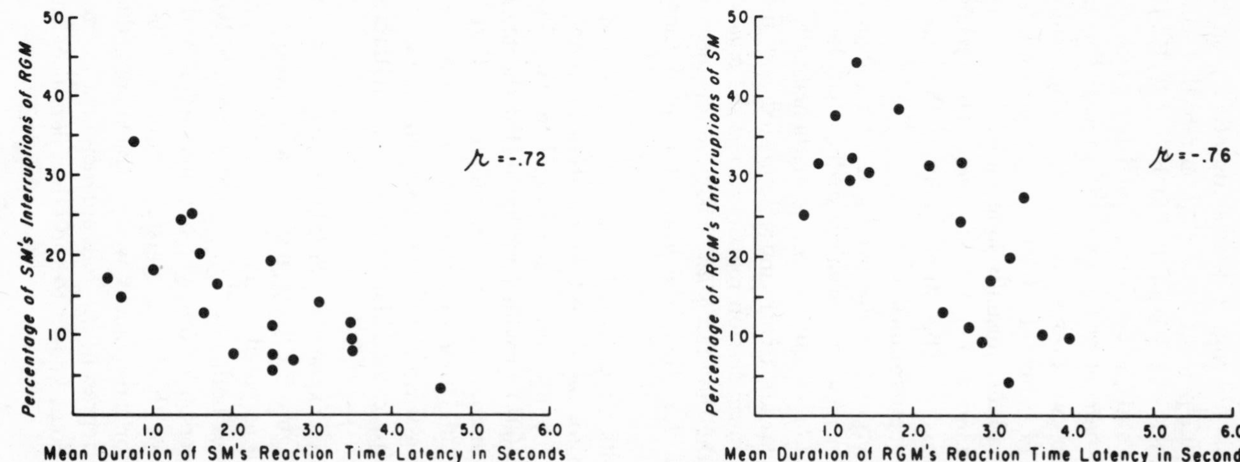

FIGURE 5.1. Left: *Scattergram of patient's* (SM) *own speech latency and own percentage interruptions of therapist* (RGM) *over a total psychotherapy series.* Right: *Scattergram of therapist's* (RGM) *own speech latency and own percentage interruptions of patient* (SM) *over a total psychotherapy series.*

single point depicting both these variables for SM in Figure 5.1, the reader should find 2.76 seconds (RTL) on the X axis and move up to 6.7 percent (interruption rate that same day) on the Y axis. Likewise, in Session 6, SM had a RTL of approximately 1.0 seconds, and she also interrupted her psychotherapist with a rate of 18.2 percent of her own utterances. The single point depicting these two events can be found by reading up directly from the RTL value of 1.0 seconds. As a third example, in Session 7 SM had an unusually long mean RTL of 4.6 seconds. She also interrupted at her lowest level (3.6 percent) during that particular session. This single point is the one furthest to the right in the scattergram.

The scattergram of the twenty resulting points, one each for the 20 sessions, clearly reveals visually what the Pearson correlation of $-.72$ (p of .001) suggests mathematically: on those days when SM was apparently most depressed and, therefore, earned her *longest* mean session reaction times she *concurrently* was interrupting the therapist *least*. Likewise, on those days when she had her *shortest* RTL she also interrupted the therapist *most frequently*.

The results on the right side of Figure 5.1 present a similar scattergram for the same two variables for therapist RGM's own concurrent latency and interrupting behavior. The Pearson r of $-.76$ (p of .001) provided evidence that the findings shown for SM have generality to another individual. Further evidence of the fidelity, and therefore the generalizability, of this crossvalidated finding was provided by a similar finding in the remaining psychotherapy cases (Matarazzo, Wiens, Matarazzo, and Saslow, 1968, Table 3).

As an initial explanation of this finding we have interpreted the results in Figure 5.1 to suggest that a *common factor* operates in this, as well as possibly many other, conversational experiences, and it defines both how long a speaker waits before answering the other person in any given conversation and how often he will interrupt this other person before he, the latter, finishes speaking. For the moment we are speculating that this common factor may represent the felt urgency of a given speaker's need to make a point known to the other person or each individual's own drive level that day or the rapport he feels for the other person or his positive regard or lack of it for the other person and so forth. Possibly the reader can offer even more likely explanatory hypotheses as to why how long one waits before he answers his conversational partner and how often one interrupts him during that same conversation are highly intercorrelated. As a point of fact, Jaffe (1968, p. 270) offers a very stimulating mathematical-psychological hypothesis for our Figure 5.1 results. His hypothesis is both heuristic and logically appealing.

Covariation of Own RTL and Other Speaker's Interrupting Behavior

The same seven psychotherapy cases permitted us to extend our search for interrelationships between variables one step further. We next searched for *cross-speaker interrelationships*. One such example is presented in Figure 5.2. The two speakers again were RGM and SM, and the scattergrams were plotted following the method described above. To construct the scattergram on the left, for each session we took patient SM's mean RTL during that session and found that mark on the X axis. We next discerned how much interrupting RGM did of SM that day and, reading up from the X axis, found this percentage level on the Y axis. At this intersection a single point depicting these two events was placed in the scatter plot, and this process was repeated 20 times (one point for each of the 20 psychotherapy sessions).

The resulting scattergrams and the magnitude of the Pearson correlations (r of $-.50$, p of .01 for SM as the reference and r of $-.65$, p of .01 for RGM as the reference) give evidence that how much any given speaker is *interrupted by another person* is to a sizable extent a function of how long or short the first person waits before answering the second speaker. On those days that SM showed her *shortest* (quickest) mean reaction time latencies, her therapist, RGM, was interrupting her at her own (RGM's) highest levels for interruption. Conversely, on the days SM contributed her longest reaction time latencies RGM concurrently interrupted her least often. The scattergram at the right of Figure 5.2 crossvalidates this finding for RGM as the reference.

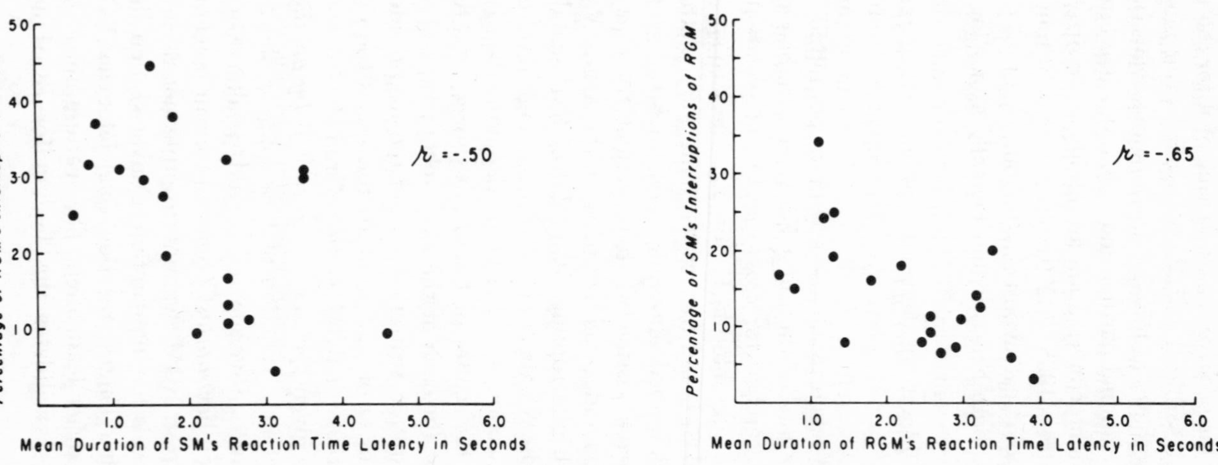

FIGURE 5.2. Left: *Scattergram of patient's (SM) speech latency and percentage of therapist's (RGM) interruptions of patient over a total psychotherapy series.* Right: *Scattergram of therapist's (RGM) speech latency and percentage of patient's (SM) interruptions of therapist over a total psychotherapy series.*

Patient SM interrupted RGM least when RGM had her own longest reaction times and interrupted her most when RGM had her shortest reaction times. (We are aware that the negative correlations equally well could mean that the duration of a speaker's latency can be the result of how often the other speaker interrupts him and will leave this cause and effect question open for future research to clarify.)

The results shown in Figure 5.2 also held up for the other psychotherapy cases studied. To our knowledge, such a finding showing a dynamic relationship between such different variables in two different speakers (the ultimate long range goal of our research program) has not been reported from any other program of research. If the finding shown in Figure 5.1 of a self-self correlation between *two* different variables and the finding of a self-other correlation between two variables operating between two speakers (Figure 5.2), and the further finding of a dynamic synchrony between the level of magnitude of a single speech variable in two different speakers can be confirmed by other investigators, this fact would appear to suggest that the search by interested investigators for still further interrelationships among and between speech variables may prove highly successful. The magnitude of the correlations for those variables discovered to date leaves little question in our minds that other investigators will confirm and, hopefully, extend these findings. In their research programs, Heller (1968, 1971); Jaffe and Feldstein (1970); and Pope and Siegman (1965, 1966 and other references) have identified still other important variables in the two-person interaction, as well as some variables similar to ours.

Relationship Between DOU and RTL

When we were still in the process of conducting our earliest test-retest reliability studies, we carried out a study in which we correlated each of Chapple's then 12 speech variables with each of the other 11 variables (Matarazzo, Saslow, and Hare, 1958). That study revealed that some of these variables were redundant and that two variables, duration of utterance and reaction time latency, were exerting the major influence in these speech measures, with initiative time latency and a variant of interruption being of next importance in the speech analyses and research we were conducting. A by-product of this 1958 intercorrelational study, however, was that we were able to discern such additional facts as (1) how long, on the average, a person spoke per utterance (DOU) was *moderately negatively correlated* with how long he waited before he spoke (RTL); (2) how often he interrupted was *not* related to how long he spoke per utterance (DOU); (3) how often he spoke (units of utterance) was *not* related to how long he waited before speaking (RTL); (4) units of utterance were not related to whether he did or did not dominate the other speaker when both speakers were speaking simultaneously.

We first reported in 1958 that DOU and RTL are negatively correlated (r of $-.27$, p of .05; and r $-.30$, p of .05 in two of our first samples of 60 different pairs of interviews). Since then Pope and Siegman (1966, p. 151) have reported a similar finding (r of $-.27$, p of .06), and this was confirmed by Ramsay (1966, p. 117), who reported finding the same type of negative relationship (r of $-.34$) and by Jaffe and Feldstein (1970, pp. 31–33) who report several additional examples of negative correlations of this same order of magnitude. This now ubiquitous finding suggests that people who talk in typically long utterances also have a tendency to answer their conversational partner with a short latency, and those individuals who are more hesitant in answering (who have longer reaction times) tend to speak in shorter utterances when they do speak. Such a finding would not surprise many people. Yet in a further beginning search for the potential existence of such relationships as these, and the others just mentioned in conjunction with our seven psychotherapy cases, we find that one or another of such relationships holds for most of the speakers in such a clinical encounter but does *not* hold for one or two of the remaining therapist-patient pairs.

This last preliminary finding is of considerable interest to us. For the past two decades psychotherapy research psychologists such as Rogers, Bordin, Strupp, Heller, Pope and Siegman, Truax, Bergin, Gendlin, Luborsky, and others have been attempting to construct measures of the dynamic phenomena in psychotherapy, such as empathy, transference, warmth, unconditional positive regard, experiencing, and other so-called "process" variables. Further research may show that the presence or absence of these common or seemingly almost universal *correlations* between our speech measures, in any *particular* psychotherapy pair, may turn out to be a highly sensitive *index* of the stage and quality of the process of this psychotherapeutic relationship. These correlations may turn out to be a sensitive measure of the depth or extent of the relationship. Independent, albeit only beginning, evidence for this belief will be found in the studies of Craig (1966), Pierce and Mosher (1967), Pope and Siegman (1967), Heller (1968), and Jaffe and Feldstein (1970). Additionally, Bierman (1969) shares our view and, in a very thoughtful review of the literature of some aspects of this complex field, offers an exploratory model and suggestion for the inability of Kiesler, Mathieu, and Klein (1967) to find the postulated relationship between their interview process variable (*experiencing*) and the concomitant interview speech measures we are studying. Kiesler, Mathieu and Klein failed to find a correlation between their own process variable, *experiencing* (as rated by judges), and duration of silence in 120 eight-minute segments of patient and therapist verbalizations. Pierce and Mosher (1967), however, found a good relationship between an interviewer's level of *empathy* (as also later independently rated by judges) and his own silence and interruption behaviors in the same interview segment. Truax (1970) has recently reported finding a similar relationship between duration of therapist talk (utterance) and his independently rated level of *accurate empathy* (as well as the patient's level of overall improvement during therapy). Therapists who talked more per session (and over all sessions) were rated (independently) as showing higher levels of accurate empathy, and their patients also showed greater degrees of overall improvement than therapists who talked less. Inasmuch as duration of utterance as a measure can be derived quickly and efficiently from a tape recording merely by counting the words in an utterance, and latency and interruption derived almost as easily, these last studies indicate that studies simultaneously using process measures from *each* of these content and noncontent systems are now possible.

SPEAKER A	SPEAKER B
Utterance Duration A B	Utterance Duration A B
Reaction Time Latency A B	Reaction Time Latency A B
Initiative Time Latency (and Initiative Utterance) A B	Initiative Time Latency (and Initiative Utterance) A B
A's Interruption of B (A dominates) A B	B's Interruption of A (B dominates) A B
A's Enclosed Interruption of B (B dominates) A B	B's Enclosed Interruption of A (A dominates) A B

FIGURE 5.3. *Schematic representation of speech measures.*

Craig's (1966) finding that the level of "congruence" between an interviewer's remarks and a patient's own beliefs also correlate with the patient's noncontent speech behavior is still another example of what we believe may before long be found to be dozens of such correlations. The research by Heller (1968, 1971) and Pope and Siegman (1967) on the influence on an interviewee's speech behavior of interviewer attributes such as friendliness versus hostility or passivity versus activity or an ambiguous (or open-ended) versus less ambiguous (more structured) interviewing style are further examples. Additionally, these latter authors have studied the effect of interviewer status (low versus high) or interviewee's clinical state (anxious versus depressed) and shown interesting correlates of these with interviewee noncontent speech behavior of the type we are studying. Although research has only been begun, these studies do, in many dimensions, serve as a beginning body of evidence relating noncontent speech behaviors similar to those we have reported so far (DOU, RTL, and interruptions) to a variety of interview variables traditionally assessed from the *content* of the same interview. This is the bifurcation in interview research we reviewed in Chapter 1.

A graphic schematic representation of each of the noncontent speech measures we have been studying in our own research follows (Figure 5.3). This schematic representation of single occurrences or examples of our noncontent speech measures may facilitate the understanding of the verbal definitions of these same noncontent measures provided in Chapter 1. These latter verbal definitions are based on *mean* values of the single occurrences schematically diagrammed in Figure 5.3.

6

Relationships between Noncontent Speech Variables and Interview Content

Our Early Attempts to Study Interview Content

One goal of our research program from the beginning was to relate the noncontent variables of duration of utterance, reaction time latency, and interruptions to indexes of the current emotional, attitudinal, or motivational states of our subjects. The findings that we have cited from the work of other investigators would clearly suggest that they have had similar goals. It is thus appropriate that in this final chapter we review our current research undertaking: a program designed to investigate the relationships among the speech variables of DOU, RTL, and interruptions to a variety of independently assessed (content-derived) motivational and personality variables characteristic of the same interviewee.

Until recently there has been a relative paucity of replicated and dependable findings regarding the underlying motivational and attitudinal states that might both be operating and mirroring themselves in changes in noncontent speech behavior. One reason for this is that there have been and are few, if any, adequate verbal content or other behavioral criterion measures against which to study the noncontent speech and silence measures. Nevertheless, few as these have been, the criterion measure most typically employed in interview and psychotherapy research has been and is content analysis. For a good introduction to the field of content-analysis of psychotherapeutic and other two-person communications the reader should consult the recent review by Marsden (1971) and the earlier classic papers he cites. One definition of content-analysis that Marsden offers is a rather broad one; that is, that content analysis denotes a research technique for the systematic ordering of the content of communication processes. This definition could subsume much of the research, noncontent as well as content, described in this book inasmuch as a major long-range goal of investigators who study either content or noncontent speech variables is to elucidate the pertinent characteristics or dimensions of these latter for understanding the emotional or motivational state of an individual.

One of our own first attempts to study the relationship of the content of an interview to the concurrent noncontent speech behavior of the interviewee was in a study by Kanfer, Phillips, Matarazzo, and Saslow (1960). This first study was not a direct investigation of the effect on the noncontent speech measures of an interviewer and the interviewee's talking about different content topics as such. Instead the study utilized an interviewer who was asked to vary his delivery or *style of speaking* (neutral versus interpretive statements) of relatively standardized content in his interviews with two groups of student-nurse interviewees. In one part of the interview the interviewer used a neutral nonjudgmental style of open-ended nondirective interviewing; in the second part (appropriately counterbalanced for possible order or sequence effects) the interviewer, continuing to talk about the *same* content, made *interpretations* about the student-nurse interviewee's motivations, life style, and so forth. The result was a dramatic and statistically significant drop (25 percent) in the interviewee's mean duration of utterance under the interpretation condition.

In our next investigation (Matarazzo, Weitman, and Saslow, 1963), the interviewer was asked to continue to employ nondirective interviewing throughout but this time systematically to vary three prescribed content areas (education, occupation, and family) for us to assess more directly the effect of such different content on an interviewee's mean duration of utterance. Although the obtained values for the mean durations of utterance of the 20 Ss varied slightly across the three content areas in this first bona fide content study, these differences were not statistically significant. Therefore, inasmuch as Chapple had guessed that, within limits, the content of an interview would not affect an interviewee's speech behavior, we interpreted this 1963 finding to mean that the speech measures we were using were stable and unchanging across many different, if not most, content-topic areas provided the interviewer used an interview pattern that itself was unchanging except for different content from period to period (for example a DOU of 5–5–5 and RTL of 1–1–1). The findings are summarized in our Figure 6.1, although the interested reader is encouraged to consult the original article for details. To allow study-to-study comparisons across our various content studies, the interviewee values for each period were converted to a common base, separately for each study, by using the content topic, education, as our standard and then dividing the mean duration of utterance value in each of the three periods by the mean value of the period in which education was discussed. This process not only yields a standard baseline period of unity (1.00) but also allows us to compare directly the relative value of the speech behavior in each of the two remaining content periods against this value of unity.

Relative to their discussion of their own education background, the mean duration of utterance of the 20 police applicant interviewees was 16 percent greater (1.16 versus 1.00) when they were talking with the interviewer for 15 minutes about their occupational history and 18 percent greater when talking with him for another 15 minutes about their family history. Unfortunately, statistical analysis in our 1963 study revealed that these differences did not meet the accepted levels of statistical significance (p of .05 or .01), so we interpreted these initial results to mean that talking about three very different content areas (educational, familial, and occupational history) did *not* alter the one noncontent speech measure (DOU) we were studying. In retrospect, it is clear that we should have replicated that study as we did with all the other studies we had previously and have since

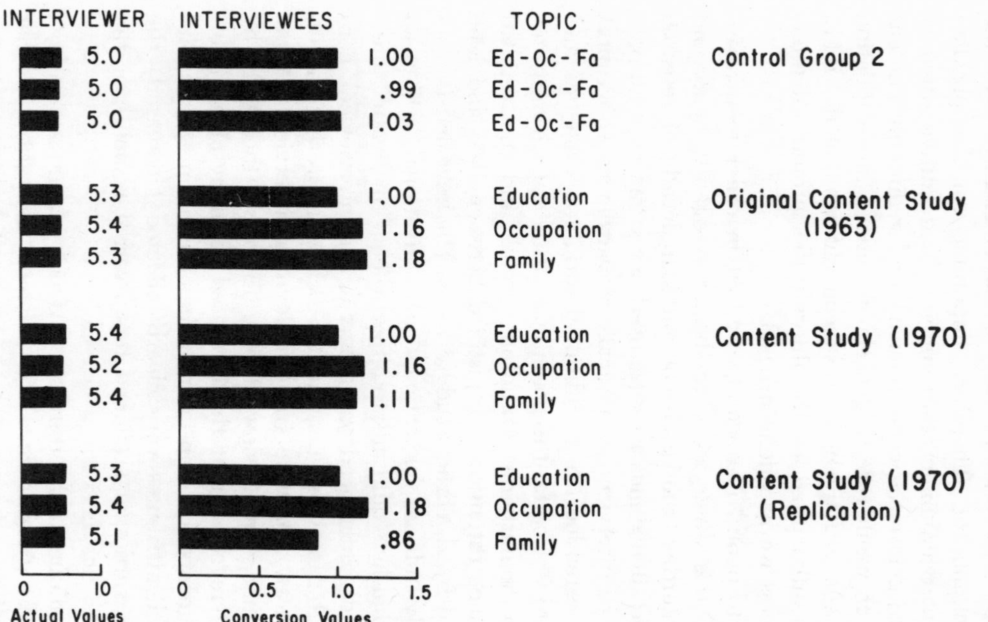

FIGURE 6.1. *Interview content and duration of interviewee—male job applicants—speech (converted to a common base).*

conducted in this research program. Nevertheless, subsequent publications by Pope and Siegman (1965, 1967) and by Craig (1966), as well as subsequent hints from our own continuing research, prompted us to reexamine our earlier findings. Both the reexamination and the theoretical importance of this problem resulted in our decision to carry out a more definitive study of noncontent interviewee speech behavior under different *content* conditions that would use larger Ns, include a crossvalidation sample, and also study all three speech indexes (DOU, RTL, interruption) rather than investigate only the duration of utterance measure as we had done in 1963.

It had also begun to appear to us that in order to increase knowledge in this whole area (for basic personality theory and study) even further, the results of our first decade of research on speech and silence measures (carried out primarily with only two samples of interviewees—patients or patrolman applicants) needed to be extended using additional variables, strategies, and interviewees to test better the potential of these speech measures as indexes of underlying attitudinal, mood, and motivational states. That such extension was justified between 1965 and 1966 was suggested by an earlier study of ours. This revealed that an experimentally induced "expectancy" or motivational "set" in an interviewee that he would talk to either a "cold" or "warm" interviewer markedly influenced one aspect of the interviewee's noncontent speech behavior (i.e., latency before answering the interviewer) in an otherwise free employment interview (Allen, Wiens, Weitman, and Saslow, 1965). Likewise, the study by Craig (1966) revealed that the increased accuracy of an interviewer's statements about an interviewee's underlying personality and attitudinal attributes very clearly affected (increased) the length of the subsequent (noncontent) verbal response of the interviewee.

These two studies and a third one (Wiens, Matarazzo, Saslow, Thompson, and Matarazzo, 1965), which demonstrated that "supervisory" versus "nonsupervisory" status was reflected in the speech characteristics of these two classes of nurse interviewee-respondents, all suggested to us that speech and silence indexes could be examined for their potential (theoretical and practical) to reveal a respondent's underlying moods, attitudes, or motivational characteristics in real-life situations. If so, that finding would be an important contribution to psychological science, especially personality theory. We thus mapped out a program of interrelated content studies, hoping to develop a methodology that we could use in real-life settings. Interestingly, our program did not get carried out as we originally planned it. Instead serendipity played a role.

Serendipitous Findings on Content and Noncontent Speech Behaviors

The basic research design of this newly planned program was to utilize the same three interview content areas (educational, familial, and occupational history) in all studies and either to create experimentally or to utilize naturally occurring differences in the motivational or attitudinal "set" of different samples of interviewees. For example, in one study we had a research assistant ask the interviewee to attempt to *deceive* the interviewer about how many years of education he actually had completed. We assumed that inasmuch as our 1963 study had "shown" that discussion of educational history would reveal values for our speech measures equal to those under the family and occupational content conditions, any resulting differences in the educational area in this new study would be a function of S's attitudinally based attempt to deceive the interviewer.

However, in this first new study (Manaugh, Wiens, and Matarazzo, 1970), and despite our methodological attempts to control for such an effect, our four groups of young college students, interviewed one at a time, showed *differential* and statistically significant changes in their speech (see Figure 6.2) and silence behavior across these three supposedly neutral content topics *even in the neutral control group* (one practicing no deception). That is, one topic (their individual educational background) turned out for all subgroups to be more salient for those *college* student interviewees relative to discussion of the two other empirically less salient topic areas (their family background and their occupational background). We used a procedure similar to that utilized in constructing Figure 6.1. Education has a 25 percent higher saliency relative to the topic, family history, (and 5 percent higher saliency relative to occupational history). The actual converted values are: family (1.00), occupation (1.20), and education (1.25).

The interested reader is encouraged to study the original report inasmuch as it had many details not shown in Figure 6.2. The latter does show, however, our unexpected serendipitous finding that education was not a neutral content area for these college student interviewees.

In a follow-up study (Matarazzo, Wiens, Jackson, and Manaugh, 1970a), also using four similar groups of undergraduate Ss but designed to remove or otherwise control for this differential educational content saliency effect, we used interviews involving discussion of two presumably (*a priori*) equally salient interview content categories for such undergraduates; namely, each S's *college major* and his *present living setting* (home, dormitory, apartment). Contrary to expectation, the overriding result of this study, consistent with that of its predecessor, was the finding, again in both the two control and both the two experimental groups, that *college major* was a content topic of statistically significantly higher intrinsic saliency (as revealed by differences in their speech behavior) for these 80 Ss than was *present living setting* (see Figure 6.2).

Concurrent with the execution of these first two studies, we also conducted and published a third study (Matarazzo, Wiens, Jackson, and Manaugh, 1970b), an extended version of our 1963 Content Study 1, in which 60 job applicants for the position of patrolman again were each given a 45-minute interview unobtrusively divided into three 15-minute segments during each of which a different content area (education, occupation, and family history) was discussed. The results, when compared with 20 additional job applicants in a control group, unlike what we thought we had found in 1963, showed that the noncontent dimensions of speech behavior of these 60 potential patrolman-interviewees also were differentially affected by the content being discussed by the interviewer (see Content Study 1970, Figure 6.1). Namely, the 60 job applicants each spoke, on the average,

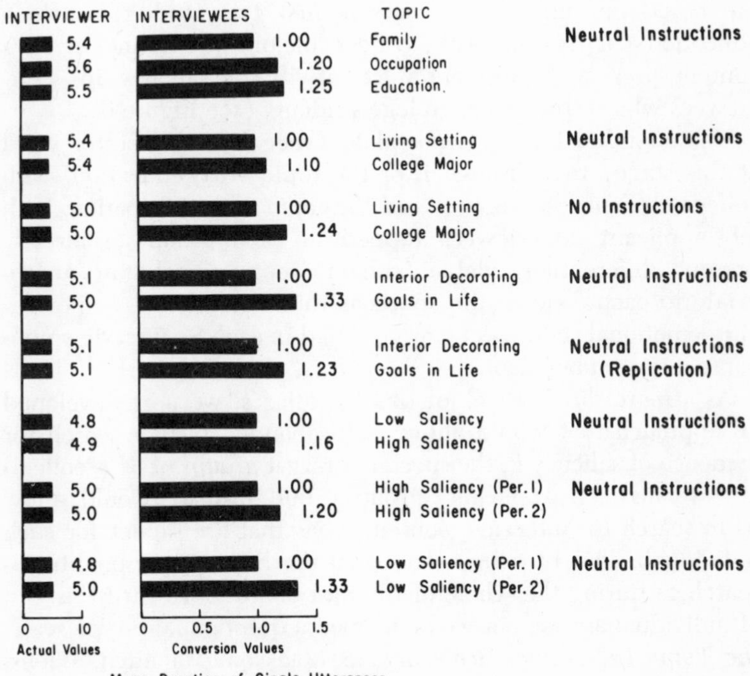

FIGURE 6.2. *Interview content and duration of interviewee–male college students–speech (converted to a common base).*

with a statistically significantly *shorter* reaction time and with a *longer* mean duration of utterance during content conditions involving a discussion of their occupational histories. These results, crossvalidated on a second or replication group of 30 similar job applicants, were interpreted to suggest that the content category, occupation, was tapping a higher level of saliency in these job applicants in this content area than was either content category education or family. This finding was consistent with the twice-confirmed finding in the first two studies in which education (or its derivative, college major) was found to be a content area with differential sensitivity or saliency in interviewees who were current college students (see Figure 6.2).

These studies led us to postulate (speculate is a better word at this stage) that discussion of the topic area, education, with college student interviewees and the topic area, occupation, with job applicant interviewees tapped in each group an already present, differentially viable (salient) motivational state appropriate to each S's own life space as this motivational or personality-emotional state was being revealed in each S's interview noncontent speech behavior.

As a more direct check of this hypothesis, we next developed an approach that would allow us to abandon further search for evidence of saliency in the speech of target *groups* of Ss ("collegiate" versus "job applicant" groups) but, instead, would allow us to search for interview content areas that are salient for each individual. This, of course, has been the hope of personality researchers during the whole of the past century. Toward this end of individual assessment we developed a questionnaire-type scale, the *Topic Importance Scale* or TIS (Jackson, Manaugh, Wiens, and Matarazzo, 1971), which we put through two refinements and which now consists of 45 items. The TIS yields a saliency score for each of these 45 items uniquely for each individual and, inasmuch as it is a questionnaire type rating scale, the TIS can be administered at any time, and the saliency information thus can be derived at a time (and place) that need have no relationship to the subsequent interview in which the speech measures are obtained. In completing the TIS, each individual is to rate on a seven-point scale the importance to him of each of 45 topic areas of the following type (although an investigator could substitute item-types reflecting any personality, motivational, or attitudinal dimension of interest in his own work):

	Low		*Some*				*High*
1. *Vietnam War*							
A. *Interested or concerned about this topic*	1	2	3	4	5	6	7
B. *Informed about this topic*	1	2	3	4	5	6	7
C. *Actively involved with this topic*	1	2	3	4	5	6	7
D. *Have strong feelings about this topic*	1	2	3	4	5	6	7
2. *Relations with the Opposite Sex*							
A. *Interested or concerned about this topic*	1	2	3	4	5	6	7
B. *Informed about this topic*	1	2	3	4	5	6	7
C. *Actively involved with this topic*	1	2	3	4	5	6	7
D. *Have strong feelings about this topic*	1	2	3	4	5	6	7
3. *Birth Control*							
A. *Interested or concerned about this topic*	1	2	3	4	5	6	7
B. *Informed about this topic*	1	2	3	4	5	6	7
C. *Actively involved with this topic*	1	2	3	4	5	6	7
D. *Have strong feelings about this topic*	1	2	3	4	5	6	7
4. *Communism*							
A. *Interested or concerned about this topic*	1	2	3	4	5	6	7
B. *Informed about this topic*	1	2	3	4	5	6	7
C. *Actively involved with this topic*	1	2	3	4	5	6	7
D. *Have strong feelings about this topic*	1	2	3	4	5	6	7
5. *Use of Drugs*							
A. *Interested or concerned about this topic*	1	2	3	4	5	6	7
B. *Informed about this topic*	1	2	3	4	5	6	7
C. *Actively involved with this topic*	1	2	3	4	5	6	7
D. *Have strong feelings about this topic*	1	2	3	4	5	6	7

In the initial form of this TIS measure of each S's areas of unique saliency, be these low or high, we used only a unitary saliency rating for each content area (item). However, as shown in the five example items above, we soon broadened this measure of "content topic saliency" by substituting for this single, all inclusive dimension the four ratings shown for each item: namely, the subdimensions of (A) interest, (B) information, (C) involvement, and (D) strength of feelings. These other 3 dimensions represent the age-old categories of knowing, feeling, and action, and any effective measure of saliency for individual use most probably will need to be broken down into these disparate dimensions.

This latter appeared especially to be the case inasmuch as correlational analysis (Jackson, Manaugh, Wiens, and Matarazzo, 1971) between the ratings given to pairs (combinations) of each of these four subscales with each of the other three revealed that our index of saliency is *not* unitary. Rather, three of the scales show high intercorrelation, one with another (level of interest, feelings, and information) and probably constitute a first factor reflecting some sort of a general cognitive (interest-information) complex from which *S* evolves or otherwise derives his saliency ratings. Conversely, inasmuch as the level of involvement subscale did not correlate as highly with these other three subscales, we presently believe it probably is reflecting a second, somewhat different attitudinal factor or dimension (an actual overt behavior or activity factor).

In our initial publication on the TIS we reported a study of the present 45-item form of it involving 348 male and 232 female college students (Jackson, Manaugh, Wiens, and Matarazzo, 1971). In addition to yielding the evidence for these presumed two factors underlying the four dimensions of our seven-point saliency measure, this study also yielded evidence that:

(1) the TIS saliency ratings show the usual and necessary levels of reliability; and
(2) the TIS saliency ratings show early evidence of being valid indexes of "saliency" as revealed by their potential to differentiate:
    (a) married from unmarried *Ss*,
    (b) draft-exempt from draft-eligible *Ss*; and
    (c) *Ss* majoring in different undergraduate disciplines.

These TIS saliency results were obtained by comparing subgroups of *Ss* differing in the ways indicated by these initial validity studies. We next decided to capitalize on and improve our newly being developed methodology for studying saliency (the TIS) in either a group of individuals (for example, college students) or any single individual, qua individual.

Saliency Study 1: Group Data

As our next study we employed a target sample or group of interviewees that we had reason to believe from the results of the initial study on the TIS would give us group results comparable to those in this earlier study. More specifically, two content areas, included among the 45 in the TIS, were selected for study: *goals in life* and *interior decorating*. We had every reason to expect that one of the 45 TIS items, goals in life, was a content area of considerably higher saliency for these collegiate Ss than was interior decorating, and thus we expected this difference to reflect itself subsequently in differential speaking behavior. In this second TIS study (Jackson, Wiens, Manaugh, and Matarazzo, 1972) a sample of 20 additional (male) college interviewees from the same collegiate population was next interviewed individually by a single interviewer in a 30-minute interview. This interview was divided by the interviewer unobtrusively into two 15-minute segments focusing, in counterbalanced order for content across Ss, in these same two content areas. Thus each interviewee spent 30 minutes in an open-ended nondirective interview discussing his views regarding his goals in life and his views on interior decorating. We found that the group of 20 Ss rated on the TIS (administered after the interview) one of these two items, *my goals in life,* with a mean saliency rating of 24.0 on our 4 to 28 point TIS saliency scale, whereas they rated the second content area, *interior decorating,* with a significantly lower (p of .001) mean saliency value of only 12.3 on the same scale. These post-interview attitudinal ratings allowed us to infer that a fairly strong *difference* in our motivational-attitudinal dimension was endogenously present in our interviewees and that this differential motivational state was made evident during discussion of these two interview topics. We thus felt comfortable to examine in this same study the effect, if any, of this inferred underlying (endogenous) differential interviewee state (saliency) on each of the three speech measures.

MEAN DURATION OF UTTERANCE (SECONDS)

It is clear from the results of this study as also summarized in Figure 6.2 that the inferred high saliency topic of *Goals in Life* did, in fact, evoke a significantly longer average duration of utterance (53.1 seconds) in its 15-minute segment of the interview than did the empirically determined less salient companion topic of *interior decorating* (40.0 seconds, p of .01). The interested reader will find these results described in our fuller report. These mean values have been converted to a common base in Figure 6.2, with interior decorating as the standard (40.0 divided by 40.0 yielding 1.00). As a further check on the reliability of this finding the study was crossvalidated in a second sample of 20 Ss from the same population. The DOU means of this crossvalidation sample were 65.0 versus 52.8 seconds, respectively, p of .05, and these results are also presented in Figure 6.2.

That we are not merely dealing with a group mean in these results was clear when we examined the individual mean DOU across the two topic areas of each of the 20 Ss in the first sample examined as individuals. Sixteen of the 20 Ss had a longer DOU when talking about goals in life, where a 10–10 split across the two topics would be expected by chance. In the crossvalidation sample of 20 additional interviewees, 16 out of the 20 Ss again spoke with a longer DOU when talking about goals in life than when talking about interior decorating.

The group means as well as examination of the behavior of the individual S thus indicate that duration of utterance, as a speech index, albeit on a beginning scale, continues to provide evidence that it can mirror or otherwise reflect content areas of differential levels of saliency. However, at this early stage it is not clear whether this duration of utterance will always be significantly larger during discussion of a salient or otherwise differentially sensitive or meaningful topic or will sometimes be significantly smaller or show a complex, albeit still significant and identifiable relationship (for example, curvilinear, or otherwise co-varying in the presence of a second or third, concomitantly present, variable). One certainly would expect such complexity to be the case if an index of speech (DOU in this discussion) is truly viable or sensitive as a mirror of motivational state.

REACTION TIME LATENCY

The means for this variable failed to differentiate the two content areas of goals in life and interior decorating under the conditions of this study. Mean values for the first 20 Ss were 3.35 versus 2.99 seconds, respectively, and for the crossvalidation sample they were 1.82 versus 1.89 seconds, *p* not significant with either sample.

MEAN PERCENTAGE OF INTERRUPTION

This speech measure also failed to differentiate the two content areas: 5.1 versus 3.0 percent; and, 6.2 versus 6.0 percent, with *p* not significant with either sample.

Thus, to summarize this study, mean duration of utterance appeared to be a reasonably sensitive index of the TIS-derived differential saliency level of goals in life versus interior decorating, but reaction time before speaking, and S's interruption of the interviewer did not appear to be. Mean DOU was a sensitive index whether the analysis was of group means, or whether the focus of interest was the individual S discussing these two content areas which the TIS ratings allowed us to presume differed considerably in their intrinsic levels of saliency.

A Second Study of Saliency: Individual Focus

In a second experiment reported in this same study (Jackson, Wiens, Manaugh, and Matarazzo, 1972), we utilized a methodology of directly studying each S's own, uniquely reported areas of differential saliency and not those of a target group of Ss as was done in this last study. Fifty additional male college students from the same population were administered the TIS in their classroom and then, some 12 weeks later, were randomly assigned to one of three interview conditions. The first condition, called by us saliency group *High–Low* (HL), consisted of 20 Ss for whom a research colleague, independent of the interviewer, had individually examined the TIS ratings on the 45-item scale and then had selected, individually for each S, one topic from the 45 topics that the S had rated *high* in saliency and one that he had rated *low* in saliency. The high- and low-content item differed from one S to another among the 20 interviewees and thus, as a pair, they were a unique reflection of each S's own reported areas of differential saliency. Before each individual interview with the 20 Ss, the interviewer's research colleague handed the interviewer a slip of paper instructing him which two topics should be discussed, in counterbalanced order, in the 30 minute interview.[1] For 10 of the 20 Ss in this HL group the order of the two topics discussed by the interviewer was HL, whereas for the remaining 10 HL group Ss the order was Low-High (LH).

In addition, we used two control groups against which to evaluate more effectively the subsequent interview speech behavior of the 20 Ss in this HL group. One control group was called the *High–High* (HH) group and was comprised of 15 Ss who were interviewed in two content areas which each S uniquely had rated *equally high* in saliency in his own life space some 12 weeks earlier. The second control group, *Low–Low* (LL), was made up of 15 Ss who were interviewed in two topic areas they, again each uniquely, had rated as *equally low* in saliency. As a further check on the reliability of our 12 weeks' pre-interview saliency measures, each S in this study was again administered the TIS immediately after his interview.

Not surprisingly given its earlier demonstrated reliability, analysis of the post-interview (as well as pre-interview) TIS ratings of these three groups indicated that we had, indeed, achieved and utilized the saliency differential we sought in the HL saliency condition group and that, as we had planned, there was no such differential in the two control groups (namely, our *HH* saliency condition and *LL* saliency condition).

In terms of its design and methodology, this experiment clearly is our most sensitive test to date of the three speech measures in that, using each S as his own control, and interviewing each S in two areas unique to him, we could more adequately evaluate the efficiency of our speech indexes to mirror this individual's own areas of presumed underlying saliency; be these two areas *High–Low, High–High, or Low–Low*, or any other combination to suit our experimental plan. The full details and results of this second part of this study are described in our fuller report, with only a brief summary of the results presented in Figure 6.2.

DURATION OF UTTERANCE (SECONDS)

As summarized in Figure 6.2, the means of 1.00 vs. 1.16 do, in fact, reveal a longer DOU for the high saliency topic relative to

1. The interviewer was not informed which was the high and which was the low rated saliency topic.

the low saliency topic for the 20 Ss comprising the HL sample. Nevertheless, these mean values (empirically 57.8 versus 50.0 seconds for the HL condition and thus again indicating a higher DOU in the high salient condition) fail to reach the usual levels of statistical significance with this small sample of 20 interviewees.

Nevertheless, our fortuitous use of two control groups (HH and LL), instead of only one such control group (see *bottom* two studies in Figure 6.2) helps to suggest that the results of this critical experiment (HL) may be, in part, an artifact of our methodology. Thus, the results indicate that, for both the LL and HH group, in *either* of which group (or both groups) we had every reason to expect *equal* means in the two topic areas (*H* vs. *H* and/or *L* vs. *L*), the particular topic that was discussed first in the two 15-minute segments of the 30-minute interview elicited a *shorter* mean DOU merely as a function of this *order*, per se. Had we found an order effect only in the HH group we could legitimately have interpreted it as, most probably, a random sampling error. However, inasmuch as this differential order effect occurred in *both* the HH and the LL groups, it is reasonable for us to infer that such an order effect *also* must have operated for those 10 HL Ss in the group of 20 Ss making up the critical HL group in which the higher saliency topic came *first* (the 10 HL versus the 10 LH Ss). Thus, utilizing the two subgroups in the 20 Ss in the HL group we carried out the additional analysis of the 10 HL interviewees for whom the H topic came first versus the remaining 10 HL interviewees for whom the L topic came first in order in the interview. The results of this subgroup versus subgroup comparison strongly suggest that the earlier presented, nonsignificant difference results for the critical 20-interviewee HL group in this study were *muted by a content sequence* (*order effect*). More specifically, for the 10 Ss in the HL group for whom the low saliency topic came first followed by the high saliency topic area (LH), the mean DOU interviewee values were L (41.8 seconds) versus H (58.8 seconds), a very substantial difference of almost 50 percent in favor of the high salient topic. Conversely, for the remaining 10 Ss in this HL group and for whom the interview started with the high salient topic (HL), the comparable mean DOU's were H (56.8 seconds) versus L (58.3 seconds), a clear masking of the sizeable difference found in the L first subgroup (LH) of 10 Ss. The DOU speech measure once again appears to show evidence that it may be a viable index of underlying motivational state. Interestingly and again unlike the DOU variable, RTL and percentage interruptions did *not* mirror the differential saliency of the two topics in the 30-minute interview. Thus, both studies suggest DOU may be a more sensitive index than are the remaining two speech measures. Further research hopefully will clarify this possibility.

The effect of content sequence or order appeared to show itself clearly for the first time in this last study. If crossvalidated on samples with considerably more subjects, this new finding that the sequence or *order* of presentation of content also can influence our DOU speech measure could then be added to the various findings that *content* per se differentially affects speech behavior. Thus it appears we are learning not only that the differential sensitivity of the content of a conversation may mirror itself in a speaker's behavior but, also, that the effect this critical (salient) content may have will depend, under some conditions, on where and when in the conversation it is introduced—specifically, under the conditions of this study, in either the first half versus the second half of the interview. The implications of such a sequence effect, if crossvalidated, would appear to be considerable for the many communications professions and the beginning sciences to which they have given rise. We hope to explore this sequence effect even further in future research, although a second instance of it already has emerged in a Ph.D. dissertation of one of our research collaborators (Manaugh, 1971). Manaugh found this sequence effect even though he used written productions as his indexes of presumed motivational state instead of spoken indexes such as our DOU, RTL, and interruption measures. Manaugh's major finding on written communications paralleled those of our speech studies.

In support of this finding by Manaugh, we already had found in one of our earlier recent studies, one that replicated a study by Mehrabian (1965), that the *written channel* of communication may be as sensitive a mirror of each S's true underlying attitudinal-motivational state as our previous and current research is revealing may be the case with the spoken channel of communi-

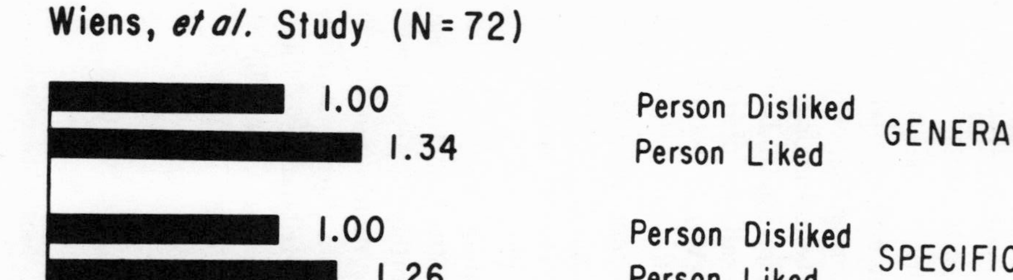
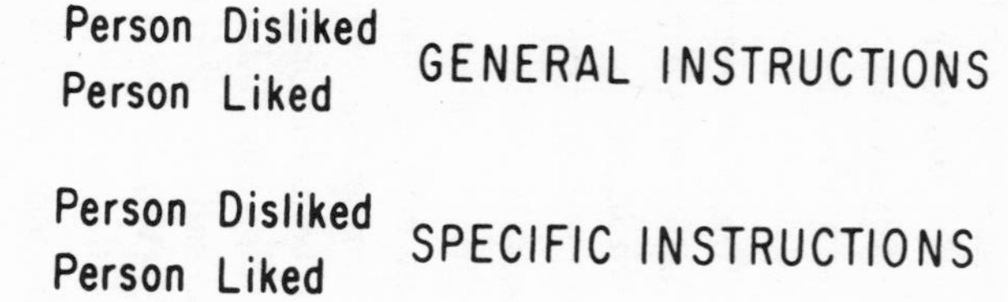
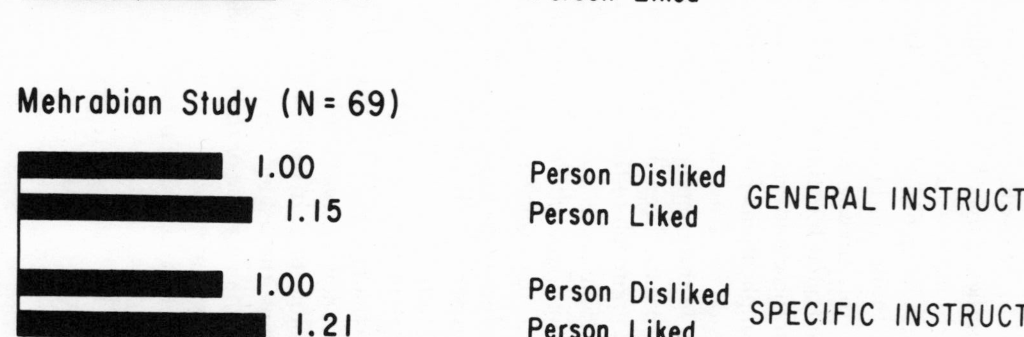

FIGURE 6.3. *Mean number of words written in a positively toned letter of recommendation by subjects under two instruction-induced attitudinal states.*

cation. These earlier results were reported in a paper by Wiens, Jackson, Manaugh, and Matarazzo (1969), and are summarized in Figure 6.3. Subjects were asked to write two letters of recommendation, both positive in tone. For one positively worded letter the writers were asked to write about a person known to them and whom they liked very much; the second, equally positive in content, letter was to be written about a person whom they also knew but whom they *disliked.* The results show that a writer will write significantly *more* words (comparable to our longer DOU) about the person he genuinely likes. The differences were statistically highly significant in all groups shown in Figure 6.3. The implications of this finding and attendant methodology would appear to be unlimited for students of personality.

It is clear that these findings will take on different meanings and have different implications for each reader or investigative team. That is as it should be. The reader probably can sense, even from the brief review in this chapter of our most recent line of research strategy, that we have been attempting to develop and refine a methodological approach to the study of the saliency of different conversational topic areas for different Ss. We have obtained merely beginning evidence from these studies that our speech and silence measures may have potential as sensitive indexes of these differentially salient topic areas. If this belief proves correct, the methodology we have been developing may have some applicability to the study of some of the psychological and psychodynamic states that have been of interest to numerous personality theorists and researchers during the past century. In this sense, then, these interview *content* studies have brought us to a conclusion comparable to that which our earlier *noncontent* studies also had and, thus, the reader can see that what started as a program of research on only one of the two major tributaries of interview research has now spilled over and encompasses both. This is, of course, what often happens in research.

References

Allen, B. V., Wiens, A. N., Weitman, M., and Saslow, G. Effects of warm-cold set on interviewee speech. *Journal of Consulting Psychology,* 1965, *29,* 480–482.

Anderson, C. W. The relation between speaking times and decision in the employment interview. *Journal of Applied Psychology,* 1960, *44,* 267–268.

Bierman, R. Dimensions of interpersonal facilitation in psychotherapy and child development. *Psychological Bulletin,* 1969, *72,* 338–352.

Brady, P. T. A technique for investigating on-off patterns of speech. *The Bell System Technical Journal,* 1965, *44,* 1–22.

——— A statistical analysis of on-off patterns in 16 conversations. *The Bell System Technical Journal.* 1968, *47,* 73–91.

——— A model for generating on-off speech patterns in two-way conversation. Paper presented at the Annual Meeting of the Acoustical Society of America, Philadelphia, April, 1969.

Cassotta, L., Feldstein, S., and Jaffe, J. AVTA: A device for automatic vocal transaction analysis. *Journal of Experimental Analysis of Behavior,* 1964, *7,* 99–104.

Cervin, V. Individual behavior in social situations: Its relation to anxiety, neuroticism, and group solidarity. *Journal of Experimental Psychology,* 1956, *51,* 161–168.

Chapple, E. D. Quantitative analysis of the interaction of individuals. *Proceedings of the National Academy of Sciences,* 1939, *25,* No. 2, 58–67.

——— "Personality" differences as described by invariant properties of individuals in interaction. *Proceedings of the National Academy of Sciences,* 1940, *26,* No. 1, 10–16.

——— The measurement of interpersonal behavior. *Transactions of the New York Academy of Sciences,* 1942, *4,* (7, Whole No. 2), 213–233.

——— The Interaction Chronograph: Its evolution and present application. *Personnel,* 1949, *25,* 295–307.

——— Quantitative analysis of complex organizational systems. *Human Organization,* 1962, *21,* 67–87.

Chapple, E. D., and Donald, G., Jr. A method for evaluating supervisory personnel. *Harvard Business Review,* 1946, *24,* 197–214.

Conger, J. C. The modification of interview behavior by client use of social reinforcement. *Behavior Therapy,* 1971, *2,* 52–61.

Craig, K. D. Incongruencies between content and temporal measures of patients' responses to confrontation with personality descriptions. *Journal of Consulting Psychology,* 1966, *30,* 550–554.

Dinoff, M., Morris, J. R., and Hannon, J. E. The stability of schizophrenic speech in a standardized interview. *Journal of Clinical Psychology,* 1963, *19,* 279–282.

Flanagan, J. C. *Speech analysis: Synthesis and perception.* New York: Academic Press, 1965.

Goldman-Eisler, F. The measurement of time sequences in conversational behavior. *British Journal of Psychology,* 1951, *42,* 355–362.

——— Individual differences between interviewers and their effect on interviewees' conversational behavior. *Journal of Mental Science,* 1952, *98,* 660–671.

——— A study of individual differences and of interaction in the behavior of some aspects of language in interviews. *Journal of Mental Science,* 1954, *100,* 177–197.

——— Speech production and the predictability of words in context. *Quarterly Journal of Experimental Psychology,* 1958a, *10,* 96–106.

——— The predictability of words in context and the length of pauses in speech. *Language and Speech,* 1958b, *1,* 226–231.

———The predictability of words in context and the length of pauses in speech. *Journal of Communication,* 1961, *11,* 95–99.

——— A comparative study of two hesitation phenomena. *Language and Speech,* 1961, *4,* 18–26.

——— Hesitation and information in speech. In C. Cherry (Ed.), *Information theory.* London: Butterworths, 1961, Pp. 162–174.

——— The distribution of pause durations in speech. *Language and Speech,* 1961, *4,* 232–237.

——— Continuity of speech utterance, its determinants and its significance. *Language and Speech,* 1961, *4,* 220–231.

——— Speech and thought. *Discovery,* 1962, *23,* (4), 36–41.

Goldman-Eisler, F., Skarbek, A., and Henderson, A. The effect of chlorpromazine on speech behavior. *Psychopharmacologia,* 1965, *7,* 220–229.

Greenspoon, J. Verbal conditioning and clinical psychology. In A. J. Bachrach (Ed.), *Experimental foundations of clinical psychology.* New York: Basic Books, 1962. Pp. 510–553.

Hargreaves, W. A. A model for speech unit duration. *Language and Speech,* 1960, *3,* 164–173.

Hargreaves, W. A., and Starkweather, J. A. Collection of temporal data with the duration tabulator. *Journal of Experimental Analysis of Behavior,* 1959, *2,* 179–183.

——— Recognition of speaker identity. *Language and Speech,* 1963, *6,* 63–67.

Heller, K. Ambiguity in the interview interaction. In J. Shlien, H. Hunt, J. D. Matarazzo, and C. Savage (Eds.), *Research in psychotherapy: Vol. 3.* Washington, D. C.: American Psychological Association, 1968. Pp. 242–259.

——— Laboratory interview research as analogue to treatment. In A. E. Bergin and S. L. Garfield (Eds.), *Handbook of psychotherapy and behavior change: An empirical analysis.* New York: John Wiley & Sons, 1971. Pp. 126–153.

Heller, K., and Marlatt, G. A. Verbal conditioning, behavior therapy and behavior change: Some problems in extrapolation. In C. M. Franks (Ed.), *Behavior therapy: Appraisal and status.* New York: McGraw-Hill, 1969. Pp. 569–588.

Holsti, O. R. Content analysis. In G. Lindzey and E. Aronson (Eds.), *The handbook of social psychology.* (2nd ed.) Reading, Mass.: Addison-Wesley, 1968, Vol. 2, Pp. 596–692.

Jackson, R. H., Manaugh, T. S., Wiens, A. N., and Matarazzo, J. D. A method for assessing the saliency level of areas in a person's current life situation. *Journal of Clinical Psychology,* 1971, *27,* 32–39.

Jackson, R. H., and Pepinsky, H. B. Interviewer activity and status effects upon revealingness in the initial interview. *Journal of Clinical Psychology,* (in press).

Jackson, R. H., Wiens, A. N., Manaugh, T. S., and Matarazzo, J. D. Speech behavior under conditions of differential saliency in interview content. *Journal of Clinical Psychology,* 1972 (in press).

Jaffe, J. Computer assessment of dyadic interaction rules from chronographic data. In J. Shlien, H. Hunt, J. D. Matarazzo, and C. Savage (Eds.), *Research in psychotherapy: Vol. 3.* Washington, D.C.: American Psychological Association, 1968. Pp. 260–276.

Jaffe, J. and Feldstein, S. *Rhythms of dialogue.* New York: Academic Press, 1970.

Johnston, G., Jansen, J., Weitman, M., Hess, H. F., Matarazzo, J. D., and Saslow, G. A punched tape data preparation system for use in psychiatric interviews. *Digest of the 1961 International Conference on Medical Electronics,* July, 1961, p. 17.

Kanfer, F. H. Verbal rate, eyeblink and content in structured psychiatric interviews. *Journal of Abnormal and Social Psychology,* 1960, *61,* 341–347.

——— Verbal conditioning: A review of its current status. In T. R. Dixon and D. L. Horton (Eds.), *Verbal behavior and general behavior theory.* New Jersey: Prentice-Hall, 1968.

Kanfer, F. H., & Marston, A. R. The relationship between personality variables and verbal response characteristics. *Journal of Clinical Psychology,* 1962, *18,* 426–428.

Kanfer, F. H., Phillips, J. S., Matarazzo, J. D., and Saslow, G. Experimental modification of interviewer content in standardized interviews. *Journal of Consulting Psychology,* 1960, *24,* 528–536.

Kasl, S. V., and Mahl, G. F. A simple device for obtaining certain verbal activity measures during interviews. *Journal of Abnormal and Social Psychology,* 1956, *53,* 388–390.

Kiesler, D. J. *Psychotherapy process research: Methods and systems.* Chicago: Aldine-Atherton, in press.

Kiesler, D. J., Mathieu, P. L., and Klein, M. H. Patient experiencing level and Interaction Chronograph variables in therapy interview segments. *Journal of Consulting Psychology,* 1967, *31,* 224.

Krasner, L. Studies of the conditioning of verbal behavior. *Psychological Bulletin,* 1958, *55,* 148–171.

——— The operant approach in behavior therapy. In A. E. Bergin and S. L. Garfield (Eds.), *Handbook of psychotherapy and behavior change: An empirical analysis.* New York: John Wiley & Sons, 1971. Pp. 612–652.

Lauver, P. J. Inexpensive apparatus for quantifying speech and silence behaviors. *Journal of Counseling Psychology,* 1970, *17,* 378–379.

Lauver, P. J., Kelley, J. D., and Froehle, T. C. Client reaction time and counselor verbal behavior in an interview setting. *Journal of Counseling Psychology,* 1971, *18,* 26–30.

Mahl, G. F. Disturbances and silences in the patient's speech in psychotherapy. *Journal of Abnormal and Social Psychology,* 1956a, *53,* 1–15.

——— A simple device for obtaining certain verbal activity measures during interviews. *Journal of Abnormal and Social Psychology,* 1956b, *53,* 388–390.

——— Exploring emotional states by content analysis. In I. Pool (Ed.), *Trends in content analysis.* Urbana: Univ. of Illinois Press, 1959. Pp. 89–130.

Manaugh, T. S. Effects of endogenously present and exogenously produced motivational sets on verbal productivity. Unpublished doctoral dissertation, University of Oregon Medical School, 1971.

Manaugh, T. S., Wiens, A. N., and Matarazzo, J. D. Content saliency and interviewee speech behavior. *Journal of Clinical Psychology,* 1970, *26,* 17–24.

Marsden, G. Content-analysis studies of therapeutic interviews: 1954 to 1964. *Psychological Bulletin,* 1965, *63,* 298–321.

——— Content analysis studies of psychotherapy: 1954 through 1968. In A. E. Bergin and S. L. Garfield (Eds.), *Handbook of psychotherapy and behavior change: An empirical analysis.* New York: John Wiley & Sons, 1971. Pp. 345–407.

Matarazzo, J. D. Prescribed behavior therapy: Suggestions from interview research. In A. J. Bachrach (Ed.), *Experimental foundations of clinical psychology.* New York: Basic Books, 1962. Pp. 471–509.

———The interview. In B. B. Wolman (Ed.), *Handbook of clinical psychology.* New York: McGraw-Hill, 1965. Pp. 403–450.

Matarazzo, J. D., Allen, B. V., Saslow, G., and Wiens, A. N. Characteristics of successful policemen and firemen applicants. *Jorunal of Applied Psychology,* 1964, *48,* 123–133.

Matarazzo, J. D., Hess, H. F., and Saslow, G. Frequency and duration characteristics of speech and silence behavior during interviews. *Journal of Clinical Psychology,* 1962, *18,* 416–426.

Matarazzo, J. D., Holman, D. C., and Wiens, A. N. A simple measure of interviewer and interviewee speech durations. *The Journal of Psychology,* 1967, *66,* 7–14.

Matarazzo, J. D., and Saslow, G. A technique for studying changes in interview behavior. In E. A. Rubinstein and M. B. Parloff (Eds.), *Research in psychotherapy.* Washington, D.C.: American Psychological Assoc., 1959, Pp. 125–159.

——— Differences in interview interaction behavior among normal and deviant groups. In I. A. Berg and B. M. Bass (Eds.), *Conformity and deviation.* New York: Harper & Row, 1961, Pp. 286–327.

Matarazzo, J. D., Saslow, G., and Hare, A. P. Factor analysis of interview interaction behavior. *Journal of Consulting Psychology,* 1958, *22,* 419–429.

Matarazzo, J. D., Saslow, G., and Matarazzo, R. G. The Interaction Chronograph as an instrument for objective measurement of interaction patterns during interviews. *Journal of Psychology,* 1956, *41,* 347–367.

Matarazzo, J. D., Saslow, G., Matarazzo, R. G., and Phillips, J. S. Stability and modifiability of personality patterns manifested during a standardized interview. In P. A. Hoch and J. Zubin (Eds.), *Psychopathology of communication.* New York: Grune & Stratton, 1958. Pp. 98–125.

Matarazzo, J. D., Weitman, M., and Saslow, G. Interview content and interviewee speech durations. *Journal of Clinical Psychology,* 1963, *19,* 463–472.

Matarazzo, J. D., Weitman, M., Saslow, G., and Wiens, A. N. Interviewer influence on durations of interviewee speech. *Journal of Verbal Learning and Verbal Behavior,* 1961, *1,* 451–458.

Matarazzo, J. D., and Wiens, A. N. Interviewer influence on durations of interviewee silence. *Journal of Experimental Research in Personality,* 1967, *2,* 56–69.

Matarazzo, J .D., Wiens, A. N., Jackson, R. H., and Manaugh, T. S. Interviewee speech behavior under conditions of endogenously-present and exogenously-induced motivational states. *Journal of Clinical Psychology,* 1970a, *26,* 141–148.

——— Interviewee speech behavior under different content conditions. *Journal of Applied Psychology,* 1970b, *54,* 15–26.

Matarazzo, J. D., Wiens, A. N., Matarazzo, R. G., and Saslow, G. Speech and silence behavior in clinical psychotherapy and its laboratory correlates. In J. Shlien, H. Hunt, J. D. Matarazzo and C. Savage (Eds.), *Research in psychotherapy: Vol. 3.* Washington, D. C.: American Psychological Association, 1968. Pp. 347–394.

Matarazzo, J. D., Wiens, A. N., and Saslow, G. Studies in interview speech behavior. In L. Krasner and L. P. Ullmann (Eds.), *Research in behavior modification: New developments and implications.* New York: Holt, Rinehart & Winston, 1965. Pp. 179–210.

Matarazzo, J. D., Wiens, A. N., Saslow, G., Dunham, R. M., and Voas, R. B. Speech durations of astronaut and ground communicator. *Science,* 1964, *143,* 148–150.

Mehrabian, A. Communication length as an index of communicator attitude. *Psychological Reports,* 1965, *17,* 519–522.

Molde, D. A., and Wiens, A. N. Interview interaction behavior of nurses with task versus person orientation. *Nursing Research,* 1967, *17,* 45–51.

Morris, R. L., Johnson, G. I., Bailey, D. D., and Wiens, A. N. A twenty-four channel temporal-event digital recording system. *Medical Research Engineering,* 1968, *7,* 406–411.

Nathan, P. E., Schneller, P., and Lindsley, O. R. Direct measurement of communication during psychiatric admission interviews. *Behavior Research and Therapy,* 1964, *2,* 49–57.

Norwine, A. C., and Murphy, O. J. Characteristic time intervals in telephone conversation. *Bell System Technical Journal,* 1938, *17,* 281–291.

Phillips, J. S., Matarazzo, J. D., Matarazzo, R. G., and Saslow, G. Observer reliability of interaction patterns during interviews. *Journal of Consulting Psychology,* 1957, *21,* 269–275.

Pierce, W. D., and Mosher, D. L. Perceived empathy, interviewer behavior and interviewee anxiety. *Journal of Consulting Psychology,* 1967, *31,* 101.

Pittenger, R. E., Hockett, C. F., and Danehy, J. J. *The first five minutes: A sample of microscopic interview analysis.* Ithaca, New York: Paul Martineau, 1960.

Pope, B., Blass, T., Siegman, A. W., and Raher, J. Anxiety and depression in speech. *Journal of Consulting and Clinical Psychology,* 1970, *35,* 128–133.

Pope, B., and Siegman, A. W. Interviewer specificity and topical focus in relation to interviewee productivity. *Journal of Verbal Learning and Verbal Behavior,* 1965, *4,* 188–192.

——— Interviewer-interviewee relationship and verbal behavior of interviewee in the initial interview. *Psychotherapy: Theory, Research, and Practice,* 1966, *3,* 149–152.

——— Interviewer warmth and verbal communication in the initial interview. *Proceedings of the 75th Annual Convention of the American Psychological Association,* 1967, 245–246.

Pope, B., Siegman, A. W., and Blass, T. Anxiety and speech in the initial interview. *Journal of Consulting and Clinical Psychology,* 1970, *35,* 233–238.

Ramsay, R. W. Personality and speech. *Journal of Personality and Social Psychology,* 1966, *4,* 116–118.

Ramsay, R. W., and Law, L. N. The measurement of duration of speech. *Language and Speech,* 1966, *9,* 96–102.

Ray, M. L., and Webb, E. J. Speech duration effects in the Kennedy news conferences. *Science,* 1966, *153,* 899–901.

Rogers, C. R. *Counseling and psychotherapy.* Boston: Houghton Mifflin, 1942.

Salzinger, K. Experimental manipulation of verbal behavior: A review. *Journal of General Psychology,* 1959, *61,* 65–94.

Saslow, G., and Matarazzo, J. D. A technique for studying changes in interview behavior. In E. A. Rubenstein and M. B. Parloff (Eds.), *Research in psychotherapy.* Vol. 1. Washington, D. C.: American Psychological Association, 1959. Pp. 125–159.

Saslow, G., Matarazzo, J. D., and Guze, S. B. The stability of Interaction Chronograph patterns in psychiatric interviews. *Journal of Consulting Psychology,* 1955, *19,* 417–430.

Siegman, A. W., and Pope, B. Effects of question specificity and anxiety-producing messages on verbal fluency in the initial interview. *Journal of Personality and Social Psychology,* 1965, *2,* 522–530.

Siegman, A. W., Pope, B., and Blass, T. Effects of interviewer status and duration of interviewer messages on interviewee productivity. *Proceedings of the 77th Annual Convention of the American Psychological Association,* 1969, 541–542.

Simpkins, L. The effects of utterance duration on verbal conditioning in small groups. *Journal of Social Psychology,* 1967, *71,* 69–78.

Spielberger, C. D. Theoretical and epistemological issues in verbal conditioning. In S. Rosenberg (Ed.), *Directions in psycholinguistics.* New York: Macmillan, 1965. Pp. 149–200.

Starkweather, J. A. Vocal behavior: The duration of speech units. *Language and Speech,* 1959, *2,* 146–153.

———— Variations in vocal behavior. In D. McK. Rioch and E. A. Weinstein (Eds.), *Disorders of communication.* Baltimore: Williams and Wilkins, 1964. Pp. 424–449.

Truax, C. B. Length of therapist response, accurate empathy and patient improvement. *Journal of Clinical Psychology,* 1970, *26,* 539–541.

Tuason, V. B., Guze, S. B., McClure, J., and Beguelin, J. A. A further study of some features of the interview with the Interaction Chronograph. *American Journal of Psychiatry,* 1961, *118,* 438–446.

Verzeano, M. Time-patterns of speech in normal subjects. *Journal of Speech and Hearing Disorders,* 1950, *15,* 197–201.

———— Time-patterns of speech in normal subjects, part II. *Journal of Speech and Hearing Disorders,* 1951, *16,* 346–350.

Verzeano, M., and Finesinger, J. E. An automatic analyzer for the study of speech interaction and in free association. *Science,* 1949, *2845,* 45–46.

Weick, K. E. Systematic observational methods. In G Lindzey and E. Aronson (Eds.), *The handbook of social psychology.* (2nd Ed.) Reading, Mass.: Addison-Wesley, 1968, Vol. 2, Pp. 357–451.

Wiens, A. N., Jackson, R. H., Manaugh, T. S., and Matarazzo, J. D. Communication length as an index of communicator attitude: a replication. *Journal of Applied Psychology,* 1969, *53,* 264–266.

Wiens, A. N., Matarazzo, J. D., and Saslow, G. The Interaction Recorder: An electronic punched paper tape unit for recording speech behavior during interviews. *Journal of Clinical Psychology,* 1965, *21,* 142–145.

Wiens, A. N., Matarazzo, J. D., Saslow G., Thompson, S. M., and Matarazzo, R. G. Interview interaction behavior of supervisors, head nurses, and staff nurses. *Nursing Research,* 1965, *14,* 322–329.

Wiens, A. N., Molde, D. A., Holman, D. C., and Matarazzo, J. D. Can interview interaction measures be taken from tape recordings? *The Journal of Psychology,* 1966, *63,* 249–260.

Wiens, A. N., Saslow, G., and Matarazzo, J. D. Speech interruption behavior during interviews. *Psychotherapy: Theory, Research, and Practice,* 1966, *3,* 153–158.

Wolberg, L. R. *The technique of psychotherapy.* New York: Grune and Stratton, 1954.

Appendix: A Sample Employment Interview[1]

Period I: Occupation

I.[2] How do you do, Mr. ______? My name is Dr. ______. Can you tell me how you happened to apply for a patrolman's position with the city of ____________?

A. Well–uh–it goes back, oh, when–I think I was a freshman or sophomore in high school–uh–I was just always kind of one of those kids any time the police were around I kind of liked to be around watching them–uh– We had–uh–when, I think I was a sophomore or a junior, we had a neighbor move in who was a deputy from ______ county and any time–Ray was his name–any time this Ray would

1. This is the transcription of an actual employment interview. It was one of 60 interviews that constituted a study (see Content Study 1970, Figure 6.1) on the effect of interview *content* on interviewee speech. Our purpose was to examine the effect of different content (occupation, family, and educational background) on the speech variables of interest to us (duration of utterance, reaction time latency, and interruption). The interviewer was completely spontaneous throughout this interview except that he was asked merely to confine each of his own comments to approximately five seconds in length, to so respond in a second or less, and never to interrupt. He unobtrusively signaled (by a light switch under his own desk) the observer on the other side of the one-way mirror when he shifted from one content category to another.

2. The letter "I" designates the Interviewer, and "A" the Applicant. Names of places and individuals, including the applicant, have been deleted or changed in minor ways to insure anonymity.

come home, we—well, I was just always kind of inquisitive—what happened today and what did you do yesterday, and of course he'd always tell us kids what he was doing. Uh—he got into Intelligence and it was just over a period of years I just kept talking to him and I guess I just became more interested in what he was doing. Uh—I then joined the National Guard. My first company commander was a city policeman and I talked to him quite a while on it, asking him just exactly what the guys do, types of hours a guy works, and everything sounded real interesting to me.

I. You say his police work sounded real interesting to you. Can you tell me some of the ways in which it sounded interesting to you?

A. Uh—work sounded real diversified, a guy getting into a little bit of everything, it seemed like. He's out of doors the majority of the time; he's directly involved with people, and I get along with people real well. I realize that in this type of job there are some people who aren't going to want to get along with you, but I like—uh—I do like working with people so I took one test for the city, it was two years ago, a little over two years ago. I didn't pass that. At the time I just wasn't really sure, anyway, and I thought it was all for the best, and I just let the matter drop. Uh—I had a little more desire to go into the county sheriff's office because I like the outlying territory a little better than just being right in downtown or in a more populated area. So it's been—well, then they changed the requirements to four years of college and I only have a little over two. I'm still going. Uh—the county did this. I—uh—had heard that the county was planning on going back to two years and I started getting more interested. In the meantime, I was real interested in the city police. I'd already—was in the process of taking some of their tests. I—uh—enrolled in a course at college last term, under a county law enforcement officer, a police administration course—and I talked to him about this, asking him about police work, telling him I was in the process of taking some tests, but I still wanted to know a little more about the police department and he says,

"Well, do you know anybody in the city department?" Well, other than my company commander I really didn't. Most—I live out of the city, and most of the guys I know are in the county. He says "Why don't you get into a county car a couple of times and go out and see what it's like?" He says "The city's going to be just about the same thing." So I made an appointment and I went out on two shifts—the night shift and a day shift. Uh—they put me in fairly active districts, where there was—it wasn't just a dead night and it had been—uh—what—what—we did that night was just as everybody explained to me, it did seem interesting, there were a lot of situations where I realized a guy had to use his head; he had to make two parties happy at the same time, and I was just a little more convinced then that that was what I wanted to do. And it's just been something that's been on my mind; it—it hasn't been a spur-of-the (clears throat) spur-of-the-moment decision. Uh—I've given it a great deal of thought over a period of years and talked to a lot of people.

I. I'm sure you have. Why don't you review for me when the first inkling that you might want to go into police work came into your mind?

A. Uh—Well, like I said, I think it was back around eighth grade, maybe freshman year of high school, sophomore, somewhere around in that area, any time there was any police activity in any situation, or in any place, uh—I kinda—gathered around, like most kids do and I was just interested in what they were doing. Uh—I always tried to get as close to any officer as I could and just listen to what he was saying and listen to what was going on with the radio.

I. In addition to this early interest in police work, what other possibilities did you consider occupationally in—while you were in high school?

A. Uh—I considered a long time going into mechanical engineering. But—uh—I don't know, I got out of high school. Uh—I went to work for Johnson Company, where they make parts. I—uh—boy, I forgot to put that down, too. Well, no,

I did get it down, didn't I? Uh—and I went to college part time and—uh—I was getting bothered by the draft so then I went into the National Guard. Well, I went six months active duty between—let's see, I left in August of '64—for my—uh—active duty—and—I came out of there, I went back to work for Johnson Company and I very seriously considered staying with them, and I liked everybody down there. They're a real nice outfit to work for. Uh—I think I was the youngest—uh—supervisor that they ever had there. I kind of fell into this spot—uh—when I got back from Fort Ord (clears throat). We worked in a—we ran a department that molded plastic parts. And there was a man directly over me, and three women, that were about—oh—45 years old and a kid my age. About that time I was only about 21—20 or 21—and—the man that was my direct supervisor was promoted out of the department and I knew the department so well and everything that went on there. They just said if you feel you can do it, you keep in touch with Bob Smith, who was my direct supervisor, and if you get any problems just get in touch with Bob. Instead of having to stick somebody else in there and retrain him all over again. Uh—so this I did and I planned on staying with it. Well, I was kind of looking into the future and they just didn't offer very much, monetarily, at all, even for the college graduates, and I was by far not near graduating from college.

I. So if I understand you correctly, you're saying that you had considerable responsibility but little pay in that supervisory position?

A. I think I was getting paid—I think it was two dollars and fifteen cents an hour, might have been two and a quarter. I can't remember exactly what it was when I left. And I—uh—well, I—at that time I was considering going into police work in the county. They only required the two years of college and this was when my neighbor was—uh—I had been bugging Ray about it, asking him about it, and he said, "Why don't you come in?" Well, I didn't have my two years then, so I was kind of going for my two years. Well, anyway, I went to Bob Smith, my immediate supervisor at Johnson Company, and I talked to Bob about it and I said "I like working for Johnson Company." I just—just laid it right on the table in front of him and said "What of my future, what's my future here, Bob?" And he says, "Well, you can have a—uh—you don't ever have to worry about being laid off," but he says, "As far as getting rich," he says, "if you don't have a college education, you're not going to get rich." And he says, "I just happen to be in a position that I fell into." This guy was, well, a real little genius, is the way I can put it, I think—uh—he was a develop—his title was development engineer. But he just said there's not much of a future, and he gave me a few situations where people were college graduates and they were barely making over 500 a month. And I just felt I could do better than that.

I. Tell me how you got into the next job that you got after you left this job at Johnson's?

A. (Clears throat) This—uh—it was kind of connected really. We had this automatic molding machine that molded these plastic parts, and—uh—right at the time I was leaving, they were going to stick me in a different area at Johnson Company because they could buy these parts out of California cheaper than what we could make them right there. Uh—there's a man named Bill Olson who makes license plates for our state, and a bunch of other states bought this automatic machine. It was a —uh—it was a real complicated machine and I knew this machine just inside and out, working with it for three years. Uh—something went wrong with it, I could tell, just bingo right off, what was wrong with it, whether it was a micro-switch that was hung up or whatever it happened to be. And he knew I was thinking about leaving, and so he asked me if I wanted to go ahead and come to work for him. And what you could do with this machine was vacuum mold anything that was made out of a styrene plastic or a polyethylene, any type of plastic that could be heated and vacuum formed. And he's—he's quite a promoter, he—uh—had a few things cooking in the fire, and

—uh—so I wasn't married at the time, I was back from my active duty, and I decided I'd go ahead and take a chance on it.

I. All right, can you review for me what happened when you took a chance and left Johnson Company and went to work with him. What happened next?

A. We—uh—you've heard of Harding and Olson, heavy equipment? Uh—Mr. Frank Harding and Mr. Bill Olson have always kind of gone into some outside businesses together. They've known each other quite a long time. So Frank Harding put up the building; it was already up, he—uh—leased the building and everything. We got everything together and these machines, and we started making—uh—we took a contract over from Johnson Company. Uh—it was making cookie trays for Archer Cookie Company. And Johnson Company had—we did this at Johnson Company when the—when we weren't making parts, because some plastic parts were seasonal. So we would mold these cookie trays. And I think we had about 250,000 left to mold. So we started molding these cookie trays, and—uh—in the meantime he was putting some other machines in there that made little metal parts. And we started making these, just a little bit at a time for Johnson Company. And—uh—then of course I couldn't go out and do any selling of these products. I ran this thing by myself; I did have another kid my age who worked with me, and he got drafted, and we finished up the cookie trays. Uh—the parts weren't enough to keep me working all day so I started working part time over at Harding and Olson. Uh—just until he got—I didn't write it in there, it was so—uh—it gets so involved . . .

I. All right, that makes no difference at all. Why don't you go ahead and tell me about it now.

A. Anyway, I started working over there part time until this Bill Olson who owned this Rockwell Manufacturing got a few more orders and got enough for me to go full time over there again. And there again I could kind of see the handwriting on the wall. Uh—this part-time job they put me in at Harding and Olson, they didn't want to put me into anything that was—uh—specialized where they'd train me and they'd—and then I'd have to leave and go back over here again, so they put me in just shagging parts. So I thought, fine. Uh—I didn't mention it, but this Bill Olson had offered me three dollars an hour to start, so when I went over to Harding and Olson, I figured I'd just keep on with this, but come to find out, here they were only going to pay me a dollar-sixty an hour. So I asked why and I just couldn't do it, and he said "Well, that's all the job pays," so I just —uh—figured I had to watch out for myself, I couldn't watch out for him. And we had a customer at Harding and Olson that I got acquainted with who owned this Pacific Logging Company, and when he found out that I was thinking about leaving, he was in the process—he was a logger—Pacific Logging Company, one of the biggest around this state. He asked me if I wanted to run a small equipment lot for them on Hawthorne Boulevard. He said, "We're going to get into equipment on the side."

Period II: Family

I. I think that's an awfully good—uh—summary of your occupational history. Now, at some point, you also got married. Can you tell me about this?

A. I got married last summer. August 26, here in town. Uh—my wife and I started going together—I was still at Johnson Company. In fact, we went—started going together in April, and I left for Fort Ord in August. She was only a senior in high school then and she went down to college, and I was down to Fort Ord until December 11th. And—uh—she—uh—says here, yeah, it was right up until December 11 and I came back and she was at college and then I went back to work for Johnson Company. We went together, up until the time we got married, fairly steady, about three years.

I. How much contact had you had with her parents, and how much close contact had your parents had with her before you married her?

A. Well—uh—I was over there quite often. Her dad—I should

say her step-dad—uh—her mother's been divorced and remarried—owns two brake shops here and—uh—I guess I am fairly mechanically inclined—mechanics comes real easy to me—and there would be weekends when he would get fairly busy and especially in the summer time during nights—he stays open til 8 and 9 o'clock at night. And I'd go down there and help him. He'd pay me a little extra money on the side. And I get along with her step-dad real well. Uh—her mother is—I got to admit—she's an exceptional mother-in-law. She's about the easiest person in the world to get along with. I don't know what the problem was with her mother and her real dad. Uh—they were divorced when I think she was about 10. And I've never really asked. I guess they just—uh—he drank, and—uh—and of course, you know yourself, some people get all hot headed when they consume alcohol. And I guess he was one of the type. They just didn't hit it off at all.

I. Tell me something about your own family and—uh—your mother and father and what your family constellation consists of.

A. Well, my dad is a commercial artist, a painter, paints trucks, letters on trucks, and—it's all lettering, in fact. And my mother works at—uh—U.S. National Bank; she's in the note department there. I've got three sisters, one's 20. She was married a year ago February. Her husband is an officer at the U.S. National Bank. She'd met him there when she worked there part time in the summer. I got another sister who's 16, who's a junior in high school and another sister who's 13, who's an eighth grader.

I. All right, now you've told me something general about the family and about your dad being a painter. What kind of person is he in terms of personality?

A. My dad?

I. Yes, I'd like to hear how you would describe your father's personality to a man like me who's never met him.

A. Well, uh—I can honestly say that in—as far back as I can remember, I've never seen him really mad—Uh—he's real easy going. Uh—he's not a real—he's not the type who goes to social functions every Saturday night, or anything like that. He—uh—he's oh, they've got just kind of a small nucleus of friends they associate with, they golf with. Uh—mainly people she works with at the bank and their husbands. Uh—my dad works—is—he's self-employed, he doesn't have any employees. Uh—he puts in a heck of a long day, but if he feels like taking a day off, he does so, goes out and plays a round of golf or whatever he happens to want to do.

I. How would you describe your relationship with him as you were growing up and as it's matured more recently?

A. Well—again I can honestly say that I've never seen my dad—uh—or can never remember my dad being—hauling off and knocking the hell out of me. He—uh—the only one time he did was when I was—uh—and he never really laid a hand on me then; I just knew he was mad. I was in fourth grade and I stole a five-cent bag of candy out of a store—and I got caught. And the man told me to go home and tell my folks about it. He even called. And so I went home and told my mom, and my dad came home that night and I know he was pretty well burned about it. Uhm—I don't think they ever expected—of course, just like every father and mother saying, "My kid wouldn't do that," but I did it. Uh—the one thing I really wish is that we could have done more together. I wish he'd of had more time for us to fish, but he's not a fisherman. He's not a hunter; I'm not a hunter myself, but I like to fish. And he'd like to play golf, but I didn't know how to play golf until last—about the last four years and then I started taking up the game myself. But—uh—I always, when my dad said—uh—he'd do this, he meant it, and I never argued anything about it. I always respected him 'cause I knew if I didn't he wasn't going to take any guff off of me.

I. All right, you've told me something about him. How about your mother? What kind of person is she? How would you describe her?

A. Well, her and I were two of a kind. Uh—we were, you might say, the type that each knew what each other was thinking all the time. Uh—we had our spats. She—uh—I'd argue with my mother where I wouldn't argue with my dad and if she'd tell me to do something I'd, well, when I was in my earlier days of high school, I'd argue back with her, and "Well, why do I have to do that," and we'd get into a few, and then towards my last couple of years of high school, especially when I left for Fort Ord, I think my mom and I became closer than we've ever become. Uh—right now we get along great. There's no problem there, there's no resent—there never has been any resentment, other than what any kid in freshman or sophomore year in high school would resent when his mother tells him, "You're going to mow the lawn," and he wants to bug out with the guys. Of course, I always had a feeling, "Why you crabby old—you're always picking on me all the time," but I've never had any hatred towards either one of them.

I. Let's pick up on this. What was the issue or what was going on just before you went into the military? I don't think I followed that.

A. Oh—uh—nothing was really going on. It's just that she worked and I went to school and—uh—I'd get off of school and if I was going to school nights or if I wasn't working nights—uh—I was either down at school doing homework or I was working on a car I had or else after I started going with my wife, I was down visiting her on weekends and—uh—I think half the problem was I was never at home enough to really—uh—get a real close relationship there. She was either working or I was working or—I can't—it's hard for me to describe when I say we were two of a kind, temperament-wise. Uh—I just really don't know how to describe it in words. It's just something my dad's always said. I've argued with my mom more than I've ever argued with my dad. And my dad has always said, "Well, your mom and you are just—you're two of a kind. You think the same, and you—and you like to argue with each other." And he says, "She don't argue with me, so she argues with you because she knows you'll argue back." I don't think I was any different from any other kid my age, arguing with their mothers.

Uh—I just don't know really how to explain it other than what I have.

I. I think you've done a good job of explaining it. Now let's talk about how they felt when you decided to get—to marry the girl you married.

A. Well, the first time I ever—uh—trying to think of the first time I ever brought my wife over. I was working for Johnson Company then and we were playing softball. Johnson would have other teams—we would have a team that would play other companies around. And—uh—I think the first time I brought my wife over was when she came to watch a game I was playing at one night, and I had to go home and change from my uniform to some regular clothes and—uh—she came in and I introduced her to my folks then. My folks have never—uh—have never—uh—criticized any girl I've ever taken out because I think all the girls I've taken out have been pretty decent girls, or I'd never bothered taking them out. Uh—my wife's got a real striking personality, and my mom just took a liking to her right away. My mom's easy to talk to, especially if I bring somebody in, she's real easy to talk to. And—uh—they just got along well from the first time they ever met. There was never any resentment there when we planned on getting married—uh—well, we were engaged probably longer'n—we were engaged longer'n we planned on being engaged because we had a car and we had a boat. She bought a car and I bought a boat. We were engaged the earlier part of—uh—August of '66 and we were planning on getting married in '67, and then the more we got to thinking about it, there was no rush. Uh—I wanted to pay the boat off; she wanted to pay the car off. We wanted to start off with a clean slate, so we did.

I. I'm sure you've recently talked with her and your mother and father about your seeking to be a policeman. What did the three of them have to say?

A. Uh—my mom knows a few of the policemen who come into the bank and the first time I ever mentioned it to her, she of course asked me, "What do you want to be a policeman for?" All the time she had seen the interest I had talking with Ray, who lived across the street from us at that time, and I don't think it was any surprise to her. And when I first met my wife I had an interest in the police force—uh—and I was planning on going with the county. And of course, any girl, I think, her age and somebody saying, "I'm going to be a policeman," the first thing they think of is the danger. And I think she was against it because of the danger at first. This goes back a couple of years. And—uh—so this Ray—his wife is probably about 34 or so—we went over there one night and—uh—we talked with Janice, his wife, and Janice says, "I felt the same way. I didn't want Ray going in because I didn't want him getting shot." You watch television programs and this is what you see all the time. Uh—she realized there's a certain amount of danger, but then in the job I've got now, I think there's more danger in the job I've got, than being a policeman. I do nothing but drive logging roads all day long and dodge logging trucks, and I'm gone away from home clear up in the mountains and I can end up going down over a bank and nobody'll ever find me for days at a time if anything ever happened. And I think she realizes now—uh—she talked to another guy—in fact, he left our business, Timber Supply, last summer—Vic Stern. Uh—she talked with Vic's wife here a couple of months ago. And Vic's wife said the same thing, "I didn't like the idea at first. Now," she says, "I like it real well."

Period III: Education

I. I think I understand how she and your mother feel about this. You mentioned earlier that you thought of being an engineer in college. Can you tell me about that?

A. Well, I was always—mechanics, I've always been interested in it. Uh—give me something to take apart and I'll take it apart to see how it works, and I've always been that way. If something doesn't work, I've always been able to take it apart and fix it, and it's just never been hard to me. It's just like this machine we had at Johnson Company. It was a thirty-thousand-dollar machine, and any half-way normal guy would know better than even to touch the thing, but if anything went wrong with it, we had to have them then—we had to have those parts or whatever was coming out of it. We couldn't wait two weeks for a guy to get out from back East. So I'd flop these wiring schematics and mechanical schematics down and look at them and just, just analyze what the heck was going on. I've just always kind of been that way; I've never had any problem in analyzing a mechanical failure in something, and I just always felt maybe this was the way I should have gone.

I. Well, now, as you look back on your high school career and your college education, have your grades suited you for engineering?

A. No—uh—and more so, my courses haven't. In high school, it was just a general academic course that we took—uh—at Washington where I went to high school, we didn't have any—any type of mechanical courses other than shop where we had sheet-metal work or plastic shop where we worked with plastics. (Clears throat) Uh—then I went to college, and what I couldn't cut was the math. Got into the advanced algebra and trig and calculus, I was lost.

I. Now let's take this slowly and go back to high school. What were your experiences in math when you were a student at Washington High School?

A. Well, we had what was called then—I was good enough at math in grade school so that I could go right into algebra in high school. And we had algebra I and algebra II. The first year you took algebra I; your sophomore year you took —uh—sophomore algebra and in your junior year, I took geometry. And—uh—I don't—let's see, I didn't take any—I didn't take any math my senior year—uh—for an elective that year, I took physical science. I only had one elective, and I took a physical science course.

I. So I can better understand your college career, what kind of an academic record did you make in algebra and geometry?

A. They were just average. I got C's in them. But I still liked it.

I. All right, are there any—uh—ideas that you have now that will better explain why you didn't do better?

A. I know why I didn't do better is—uh—when I was a sophomore, when you look back on it, of course, it's too late, when I was a sophomore, I had a car. And that killed my grades. I was more interested in that car than I was sitting down doing homework. My mom and dad had just talked until they were blue in the face and I was just a typical high school punk, that I didn't—I didn't see the importance of high school like I do now. And I was more interested in going out working on that—I had to have a car because my next-door neighbor had a car, and, of course, when you buy a car at that age, you buy a junker. And all I was doing was working on it—take things apart and fix 'em even if they did work. And I think that hurt my grades worse than anything—was having a car. There's no doubt in my mind about it.

I. You told me you received average grades in math. What were your grades in some of the other subjects you took?

A. My freshman and sophomore year—uh—when I look back —my freshman year I remember in English—I always got bad grades in English because I—we had a lot of reading and I couldn't—If I tried to read fast I couldn't—comprehend what I was reading. If I read slow, I didn't get enough done and I was always behind. It's one thing I always thought they were lacking in grade school and high school, was teaching a person how to read. I never, never had a reading course at all, never did. Never was there anyone who taught us how to read. Uh—I'm not saying it was anybody else's fault. Uh—it sure was half my fault, or probably the majority my fault for not concentrating. Uh—but I just couldn't seem to get interested in some of the books we were reading. And I could sit and read, I could read a paragraph or a page and then I'd be done with it and then I'd go back and look at it and I'd be darned if I could remember what I'd read and I'd end up reading that same page again. Sometimes I'd read a sentence two or three times. Just because my mind was off somewhere else thinking about something else. I wasn't interested in what I was reading. And it was the same in a lot of history we had. I just couldn't get a liking to it. I tried and I just couldn't. And–uh–in my sophomore year–no, that was English. Of course, in shop, I got A's in it. Gym, I got A's in–and what else I had. Oh, I had a–uh–my freshman year, I had a Spanish course and I always wanted to take Spanish. And the teacher I had, I disliked her so bad I didn't want to study. So my sophomore year, I had shop again and gym and then a commercial art course. And all three of those, I either got A's or B's in. English again, I'd get behind in reading. I just couldn't keep up and we'd have a test and I'd be behind. Uh–trying to think. Uh–we had history. I'm sure we had history then. Uh–I think it was the same thing for that, any place we had reading, I'd get behind on that. And then at the end of my sophomore year, I began to go with a girl who kept getting A's and B's. Always felt kind of ashamed of myself, that she was getting A's and B's and I was getting D's. I don't think I ever–I never flunked a course. I never flunked a course in my life. Well, I did too, at college, but as far as grade school, I didn't flunk a course at all. And–uh–for high school and–uh then my sophomore and junior year I just–I started to wake up a little bit–or my junior and senior year, I'm sorry–I started to wake up a little bit and here she was cracking out–this girl I happened to be going with–she's cracking out grades that were making me look silly. And so we did a lot of studying together. Well, we'd go to the library and study and I wasn't working on my car all the time. And it was one of those deals, it was an excuse for us to go out but we would go to the library and we would study. She was the type who–that was what she was going for was to study, and I'd end up studying, too, and I think my grades got to be a little better. And in my senior year, English, I got–I got only C's in, it was going back to my senior year, too. History, I had a professor named Mr. Jones, and he made it a real challenge. And if I could ever take a college course from that guy, I'd take a college course from him, because I got—I think I got B's except for one. We had six grading periods and I think I got B's except for one grading period from him. And he just really made me want to work. And the same way in English. I got so that I was making myself read a little better, a little faster, and becoming more aware that—of graduating, not saying to heck with it all—wasn't the right attitude, because I knew a lot of people depended on these grades and then I started making up my mind I wanted to go to college and—uh—I realized with a low GPA I wasn't going to get into college.

I. That takes us to the next point. Somewhere along the line in high school, near the end, you decided to go to college. When was that?

A. I think it was—uh—I think it was around my senior year when I really made up my mind, but I didn't know what I wanted to pursue—uh—I was going to just start taking the general courses, the—uh—lower-division courses and hope that somewhere along the line I'd wake up and try and find—get my nose pointed in the right direction, but I think it was around my—the middle of my senior year, the first third of my senior year because everybody else was talking college and I realized that—that college wasn't just some place you go for spending your time, that I realized how important college was then, as far as making a future for myself. That just about any place you go, uh—without a college education any more you can't get your foot in the door.

I. Then you graduated from high school and started college. Can you review your experience in college for me?

A. Ah—I started going at night, to night school, because I went to—I went to work for Johnson Company by day, and I think I took 12 credits at night. I take that back; I only took six hours my first time and then I—the next term I took 12 hours. And I kept taking 12 hours until I went to—until I went in the Army. Now, the courses I took, of course, we had to take English comp. I got B's in it. I think I got one C out of it. There's three terms. I think two terms I got B's and the third term I got a C. I–I can't remember exactly. But I had a guy who made it so interesting that–uh–I looked forward to going to the class. I was taking an accounting course that term and I just got a C in accounting and then the next term, of course, it was second term English and third term English and second and third term accounting. And–uh–then the job at Johnson Company before I was supervising full time there, it worked out to where I could start going to school in the morning and work from twelve-thirty in the afternoon on until five at Johnson Company, so I started taking 12 hours then. And–I took business courses, management, production, marketing, and some more accounting courses. Then I went in the Army. And I came back out of the Army and I went back to night school and worked full time in the day. Think I only took six or nine hours at night. That's the way it's been going ever since.

I. I see you've really carried on a job and college at the same time. How would you summarize your academic record?

A. Grade-wise?

I. Yes. I'm interested in what your grade, your overall grade point record . . . (Applicant interrupted Interviewer here.)

A. In college, I think it's just a little above a C average. Uh–I think my high school was just a C also. Right on the nose if I remember right. It hasn't been anything to write home about. Uh–a lot of the courses that I took, I just couldn't get myself to sit down and read some of these books that we were having to read. Uh–in my freshman and sophomore year, my grade point was way down, and my junior and senior year in high school brought it up a little bit, and I think I just made the C average.

I. All right, Mr. ______, I believe I know something about your background. We'll soon have scored all your tests. Those test results will now be more meaningful to me after this interview I have had with you. Thank you very much and good luck with your application.

Index